Dearest Sneha,

Let Gentleness, etiquette, common sense and style never go out of fashion in your life! Live life being sensitive to others and displaying grace in all you do.

Love always
Mom
Dec 2018

The
GOLDEN
CODE

MASTERING THE ART OF
SOCIAL SUCCESS

RUKSHANA EISA

Foreword by
Shweta Bachchan Nanda

Visit us at www.readersdigest.co.in
and...

– Read latest articles
– Inform us about your Change of Address
– Request free replacement for a missing copy
– Meet our lucky Prize Draw winners
– Subscribe or gift a subscription
– Post other requests, report problems, give us your opinion

Or write to us at
Customer Service Cell
Reader's Digest
(A division of The India Today Group)
B-45, Sector-57, Noida, U.P.-201 301.
E-mail: rdcare@intoday.com

FOREWORD

In a shrinking world, where anything is accessible with the push of a button, we sometimes dismiss manners and etiquette as fussy relics of an era gone by. But manners never go out of style, ever. Take that as a gold standard and you will not go wrong. Etiquette goes far beyond pulling out chairs and holding open doors, for example – what to wear to a black-tie dinner? How late can you RSVP? Should you split the bill at the end of a date? Or how can you politely tell somebody they have something stuck in their teeth during a FaceTime call? All fall under its purview. If you are trying to navigate today's world of hyper socializing and let's face it, people are now that much more accessible and therefore that much more in your face, you would do well to learn the rules of the game, so who better to guide you through the rigmarole of social dos and don'ts than Rukshana!

Rukshi, as Rukshana is known to her friends, is unflappable whatever situation she finds herself in. Whether it be a sangria emergency or last-minute house guest, she knows how to handle the situation with grace and, most importantly, tact. A gracious hostess, and an even more gracious guest (which are few and far between these days) she has the ability to be charming while making her point, all this with a smile on her lips under even the most trying situations, and I have been through a couple with her, so I would know.

Trained in the hospitality business she has whipped many a Miss India into shape, it was about time she put her expertise down on paper so we could reap its benefits. Anecdotal and interactive, her book is a must-read! Think of it as an encyclopedia on everything etiquette because as they say, "You never get a second chance to make a first impression."

Shweta Bachchan Nanda

CONTENTS

INTRODUCTION

was with my daughter enjoying a fun mother-daughter meal at a fast food joint, many years ago. I had just opened my grooming school and my daughter was six years old at the time. We were enjoying our burgers, when a formally dressed man wearing a tie, tapped me on the shoulder and said, "Excuse me, this is my seat. I just got up to talk to my friend. Can you get up?" For a couple of seconds, I was too shocked to say anything. When he continued to stare at me, waiting for me to vacate the chair, I shook myself out of the utter bewilderment and got up. I did that not because I was at fault – I wasn't – but because I know how to behave with another person in public. Here was clearly an educated man and with everything that life and books had taught him, and he still didn't know how to behave appropriately with a woman, and that too in public.

All of this boils down to just one word – etiquette. Etiquette is a set of manners and rules that are followed in a social or professional setting. It involves an attitude of respect toward yourself and others to ensure that you and everyone else feel valued. It is about the interactions we have each day with family, friends, strangers, customers and co-workers. It is not a stuffy set of outdated rules or skills reserved for tea with the Queen.

Good manners and a well-groomed personality are an extension of good etiquette. Regardless of your age or position in life, good manners are life skills. Some people tell me that etiquette no longer matters and that the rules for good behaviour are old-fashioned. But good behaviour and manners are eternal. You will always remember someone who treated you with respect, won't you? Their good behaviour, especially when they are a stranger, leaves a mark. Many people see etiquette as snobbery. They view polite behaviour as a sign of weakness. In the workplace, people believe that it is impossible to get to the top while being polite, and that you need to be a cutthroat all the time. But this is just not true! In fact, the opposite is. Grace helps you win the race of life. Etiquette matters today as it always did. It has not gone out of style. If you want to learn more about how to practise etiquette in public, start practising it in private. It is difficult to switch on good behaviour only when you feel like you need to. Etiquette should be an extension of who you are. What we do in private defines who we are in public.

A common wall I encounter is when people say that they have bigger worries in life; etiquette, especially when it comes to appearance and entertaining, is too frivolous an idea for them to be bothered about. A woman once told me, "I worry more about catching the train on time and earning a salary than about impressing a bunch of people I don't even care about." Well, while I agree with her, this is a good example of how people get the meaning of etiquette completely wrong. The purpose of etiquette is not to put on a show for the benefit of others. Etiquette is not about air-kissing. Being polite is not just for the elite, for formal events, or the boardroom. Good manners are required everywhere, every day. Everyone should know the right way to behave in any situation. Whether it is following the dress code or ensuring that you follow the rules of standing in a queue. Manners are not just for a select few. Common courtesies like standing in a queue, coughing and sneezing into your hand – these are things everyone can and should do. Treating people well takes the sting out of everyday stress.

A friend once told me about an article in the *Reader's Digest* a few years ago, that observed how India was among the world's rudest countries. She was genuinely offended. "How could they judge India based on Western standards of manners?" She wanted to know. That's what she was more worried about. I was shocked at her attitude. What she said made absolutely no sense – good manners are a basic human requisite; the country does not matter! Common courtesies are increasingly missing from our culture. From cutting the queue at airports and ticket counters to breaking our already loose driving guidelines, for example, not halting at

> Etiquette is not about air-kissing. Being polite is not just for the elite, or for formal events, or the boardroom. Good manners are required everywhere, every day.

a red light, selfish behaviour and lack of common courtesies can be seen everywhere in our country. Whereas in other countries, it is common etiquette to hold the door open if someone is coming behind you. You never slam the door on their face. But that's not the case in India. And, when you do hold the door for someone, what are the magic words to be used? You would think they would say 'thank you', but you will be surprised at how many people just don't do that. Instead, they just waltz through. It is because of such people and their continued ignorance that a profession called 'etiquette expert' exists. And boy, do I have a job! In our hurry to be the first, we forget our manners and end up being impertinent. I understand that everyone has busy schedules. But that does not mean you forget the basics of human decency. Words like 'please', 'thank you' and 'may I?' seem to have disappeared from our vocabulary. This happens even at home. Just because they are your family doesn't mean you don't thank them for the things they do for you. What you learn at home is what you are going to do outside. Everyone wants to be a role model. So why not be a role model for how a decent human being should behave!

WHY WE NEED ETIQUETTE

Etiquette is the way you talk, the way you walk, the way you dress. Yes, some elements of etiquette deal with which fork to use to eat dessert and your tone and behaviour at parties. But etiquette, in general, is a much broader issue. It is not just about behaving well in public.

It is about behaving the same way with a rich as well as a poor person – someone who can do nothing for you in return.

> It is not just about behaving well in public. It is about behaving the same way with a rich and a poor person – someone who can do nothing for you in return.

Etiquette increases your self-confidence and gives you assurance in knowing and doing the right thing in any social situation. It ensures you are never nervous or doubt yourself. Knowledge of basic etiquette gives you the confidence to socialize with all kinds of people and shows you how to make that important successful first impression.

I always say that the first impression is made in the first three seconds. You walk into a room and within a few seconds, everyone has sized you up. Of course, that opinion changes when you spend time with them. But when you meet someone for the first time, what are you looking at? The way they are standing, how they are dressed, good manners, facial expressions... When someone looks at you, he or she should think, 'I want to be like that person.' You rarely get a second chance to make a good first impression.

Etiquette also tells you how to groom yourself. It tells you what the appropriate outfit is for a date, an interview, a cocktail party and a business lunch. Job opportunities, relationship possibilities, and invitations to parties and other social events are all inextricably linked to how you present yourself to the world.

It teaches you how to show respect. Good manners define you as a person, while etiquette is what makes you socially acceptable. We all know that we should treat others the way we want them to treat us. And respect given is respect earned. That is why if you treat others with respect and acknowledge them, you are more likely to be respected and trusted. With the measure you give, it will be measured and given back to you.

TO THINE OWN SELF BE TRUE

Ever since I was a young girl, people who were the centre of attention because of their poise, charming mannerisms, impeccable appearance and interesting conversational skills in any environment, have fascinated me. I remember reading an advertisement that stuck in my mind, which said, 'Be a model or just look like one'. I knew in my head that grooming and styling people to their full potential and teaching etiquette was a direction I would eventually gravitate towards.

This books deals with the correct social graces in different scenarios. It deals with etiquette in three parts: communication in your personal and professional life, the three aspects of personal grooming, and etiquette in the context of travelling and entertaining.

How you behave at your workplace can literally make or break your career. About 85 per cent of professional success is due to soft skills, such as social and people skills, and just 15 per cent is due to technical knowledge and skills, according to three separate research projects by Harvard University, the Carnegie Foundation and the Stanford Research Institute. Proper use of social and business etiquette always gives you an edge. A lapse in etiquette may offend the person you are interacting with and could result in the end of your friendship or may even cost you your job. While travelling, it is important to be acquainted with the culture of the place, as each country has its own set of rules to judge personal behaviour in society... all of this patiently awaits you in the pages ahead.

Remember the movie *The Devil Wears Prada*? Anne Hathaway's character goes to work on her first day at *Runway* fashion magazine in a frumpy sweater over an ill-fitting skirt. She didn't understand that you have to dress according to your environment. You will not wear shorts to a wedding, would you? Or jeans and T-shirt to a job interview. Anne's character realizes that soon enough and dresses as an employee of a fashion magazine should. She was much more confident when she dressed right, but continued to remain the same person.

Similarly, we can never underestimate the power of good grooming. Clothes really do make a man. Wearing the right outfit for the right occasion, making sure it is clean and ironed, taking care of your skin, hair and nails – all of this is more important now than ever before. Our clothes make a huge difference about what people think of us. The assessments that people make in the first few seconds of seeing another person go way beyond how well you are dressed and how neat and tidy you may look. We may think that fashion is just an indulgence and our sunny personality and kind nature will eclipse our unkempt attire. This could not be more untrue. What we wear speaks volumes in just a few seconds. Dressing to impress is really not needed, but you always have to be well put together. No matter how little we possess or how we feel on any given day, getting up, dressing up and getting out into the world is the best tribute we can give our Creator.

Yet, in the midst of all this, don't forget to be true to yourself. What we are on the inside eventually reflects on the outside. None of the world's manufacturers have invented a fabric yet that can veil your or my true character. So you see, this book is not just about altering your appearance and propagating looks over substance and character. It's about realizing the best part of you and showcasing the best version of you to the world. You already know everything that's about to follow. I am just bringing it to the fore by reinforcing these qualities. *Be your best self!*

Shining through in every situation can enhance your life in so many wonderful ways. And this book will show you how. Life is rough and tumble, so let's make it easy for everyone concerned by releasing the basic goodness inherent in each of us. I trust that the simplicity of the pages ahead will become your handbook for the days ahead in your charmed life. It is the little things that make the big difference, dear reader; we don't trip over mountains, but over pebbles. Our attitude, our temper, our tongue can be our worst enemy. Our manners only manifest what's inside our hearts.

I pray that this book holds you in good stead and like a faithful friend; no matter what the situation, day or night, always reminds you that grace wins the race of life.

COMMUNICATION

1
BODY LANGUAGE

The most important thing in communication is hearing what isn't said.

— Peter F. Drucker, author & management expert

One of the most important points to remember when you're talking to someone – whether it's at an interview, on a date, or with a stranger – is that your mouth is not the only thing that is speaking. Your body is doing some of it too. A person's body language says a great deal about how they are feeling and what they are thinking.

Studies have shown that 70 per cent of our communication is achieved nonverbally. And people tend to rely on the other person's body language more than on what they actually say. That's because your mouth can lie, but your body cannot. The way we sit, how fast we talk, how close we stand, how much eye contact we make – all of these send strong messages. These messages don't stop when you stop speaking. Even when you are silent, you are still communicating. Many times, what comes out of our mouths and what we communicate through our body language are two very different things. When faced with these mixed signals, the person you are talking to has to choose whether to believe your verbal or nonverbal message. And, they're more likely to choose the latter because it's a natural, unconscious language that showcases your true feelings.

We always believe what we see far more than what we hear. I had read about an incident that shows this is true. In 1960, when John F. Kennedy and Richard Nixon were both running for the US presidential elections, both candidates spoke well during a TV debate between them. But in a poll conducted the next day on who had fared better, there were completely different results between the TV and radio audiences – between those who had seen and heard the debate and between those who had only heard it. The radio listeners were convinced that Nixon had won the debate because his arguments were clear. While TV viewers were sure that Kennedy had won because he came across as likeable and believable. People believed Kennedy more – they bought into his body language and the signals he gave off – and did not trust Nixon from his body language.

> Everything you do with your body sends out a message. Good body language creates an air of confidence and positivity.

Everything you do with your body sends out a message. Good body language creates an air of confidence and positivity. It puts others at ease. Most people don't know this, but the correct way to stand is with your shoulder and back straight, with the stomach tucked in, as if someone has put a thread through your body and pulled you to your full height. When someone is standing straight and tall, they exude confidence. No one will know you are nervous and have butterflies in your stomach because you are telling them you are confident with your posture. I always stress this point when I train the Miss India contestants for their pageants. When they are standing in front of thousands of people, and the host asks them questions about, say, world peace, they don't need to give a complicated answer. By just standing tall and looking confident, they can say something very basic and it will make an impression.

The way you listen, look and move tells the other person whether you care or not, if you are telling the truth, and if you are actually listening to them. When your body language matches up with the words you are saying, it increases trust, clarity, and rapport. For example, when you are listening carefully to a friend talk about a certain crisis in her life, look at how your body is, too. You will probably be at the edge of your seat, leaning towards her, and sometimes, with your hand on your chin. That shows that you are listening keenly as opposed to merely nodding and making the right sounds at regular intervals. Similarly, when your nonverbal signs don't match your words, they are likely to create tension, mistrust, and confusion.

Your body should express as much as your mouth does. For

instance, if you say, "This has been a terrible day," this would probably be taken at face value. But if you said, "This has been a terrible day," followed immediately with a smile and a wink, everyone will assume that it has actually been a great day.

To become a better communicator, it's important to become more sensitive not only to the body language and nonverbal cues of others but also to your own.

Recently, a financial company called me to conduct an etiquette seminar. I was meeting the HR executives when a man walked into the room. He was sloppily dressed, spoke rudely to his colleagues, and had absolutely no manners. When I extended my hand for a handshake, he barely touched mine and quickly walked away. He said only a few words, which is not a bad thing, but the way he conducted himself was abominable. I was put off by his behaviour. I wanted to tell him, "You are asking me to train your staff, sir. But you need the training yourself." How could he ever expect his staff to want to be him? He could never become a role model for his juniors. This is a great example of how not to behave in public.

HANDSHAKES

The universal form of greeting people is the good old handshake. A study at the University of Iowa in the US found that people who start job interviews with a firm, strong handshake are always perceived in a more favourable light than those who have a limp handshake. Studies have also shown that the amount of rapport you get from a handshake is equivalent to three hours of face-to-face time. Good hand-shakers are seen as being more extroverted, and eventually, more hireable. Your handshake should neither be bone crushing nor limp. The former shows you are an aggressive, dominating person. The latter shows you have a weak personality. A limp handshake will get you the tag of a wimp and a clammy shake of a slimy one.

A good handshake means it should be firm and should last for about three seconds with two to three pumps. Extend your hand forward, grip and withdraw after a few seconds for a new acquaintance. It should be a little bit longer for someone you have met before. In an ideal world, that would be enough. But there are some people who hold on to your hand for much longer. I have seen people carry on full conversations while holding on limply to the other person's hand. If that happens to you, smile sweetly and take a few steps back. That way, the other person will be compelled to break the contact. If you lean forward even though you want to step back, you are sending out a wrong message. It's all about how you conduct yourself. I always tell the girls I train for pageants that you may be wearing the skimpiest of clothes, but if you conduct yourself with dignity, no one will be able to take advantage of you. Similarly, if you are the recipient of a bone-crushing handshake, immediately withdraw your hand. The reflex action will send the right message.

A common question I am asked is, who extends their hand first for a shake: the woman or the man? A handshake is gender-neutral. Anyone can initiate one. But even as I say this, always use your common sense. Some people may not want to shake hands, probably because it involves touching someone of the opposite gender. You must have noticed this many times, that in India, an elderly person may not be aware of what a handshake is. In that case, a simple *Namaste* is the answer.

Always remember...

A handshake should last just two to three seconds. Don't hold on to it longer than that.

A firm handshake will take you places. Make sure yours is not limp or clammy.

EXCHANGING BUSINESS CARDS

Business cards are the staple of corporate success. They are, however, an often underestimated and underplayed part of networking. The number of people who don't know the etiquette of exchanging cards constantly amazes me. Here are a few things to remember:

1. Your name and company name should be very legible. Choose a clear, bold font, and place your name and logo in a way that it has maximum impact.

2. Don't leave your home or office without carrying plenty of your business cards. It's very unprofessional when people say, 'I just gave out my last card' or 'I'm sorry. I didn't bring any with me'.

3. A business card is not just a piece of paper; it's an extension of your professional self. That is why it should be neat and tidy at all times. Once you have taken leave of your business contact, your business card is the only thing left representing you and your work. Keep them in a case or a folder that protects them from wear and tear. You get some great ones online. A crumpled or soiled business card makes a very poor first impression and conveys lack of preparation.

4. Know where your business cards are at all times. No one is interested in watching you go through your jacket and pants pockets, or every nook and cranny of your office bag or purse while searching for one.

5. Do not hand out your business card to everyone you see. Be discreet about it. If you keep distributing them to everyone, it shows your card, and in turn you, is not worth much. Also, handing out many business cards doesn't mean all those people will get in touch with you. In fact, it probably means you will get zero calls because you have not taken the time to get to know and connect with any of the recipients of your cards.

6. Business cards should be handed out with both hands, facing the person, at the beginning or end of the interview or conversation. When offered someone else's card, take a moment to glance attentively at it before putting it away.

> Send a LinkedIn connection request and a follow-up email after exchanging cards to remind the person of your mutual interests.

The giver may have spent time, as much time as you have preparing your card, so your appreciation goes a long way.

7. Keep your business cards up-to-date. When any of your contact information changes, ask your company to issue you new ones. Don't give someone a card with handwritten changes, or write on it in front of someone.

8. Never leave a business card you have received lying around you and walk away. That is extremely insulting and says you think the people they belong to are not important enough.

Exchanging someone's business card serves no purpose unless you actually use it. It is meant for following up on the initial meeting. Send a LinkedIn connection request and a follow-up email after exchanging cards to remind the person of your mutual interests. After all, the main purpose is to facilitate new relationships. When you start with a solid, polite foundation, relationships are easier to build.

> ### Always remember...
> Hand over your business card at the best possible time, either at the beginning or the end of the meeting.
> When you receive one, thank the person, appreciate the gesture and always take it with you when you leave.

PERSONAL SPACE

Every culture has its own definition of personal space and physical proximity. Westerners find the Chinese and Indian personal comfort zones too close for comfort. Instinctively, Westerners may back away when their space is invaded. On the other hand, the Chinese may move a step closer. Whichever culture you belong to, it's universally accepted that each individual has a personal space that remains thus.

Traditionally and culturally, we have lived in joint families where personal boundaries have somewhat been erased. Times have changed though and maintaining your personal space is regarded as a necessity. A three-foot radius or an arms' length is the defined boundary that should be maintained when in any crowd. Lean in to hear a quiet person more clearly, but then back away to speak yourself. One important consideration is also height differences. Stand far enough away so that the other person doesn't have to look up or down at you.

Invasion of personal space has become a growing problem in India's over-populated cities. Touching someone who you don't know very well is never welcome. I have seen some people get carried away when they laugh and they slap their hands on anyone who is standing next to them. This is clearly a no-no.

Between smartphones and other tech gadgets, it is easy for us to become completely out of sync with our surroundings. Be aware of where you are, who is next to you, and in what direction you are going.

Also, when you are talking to people, do not get too close. You will know you are too close when the person backs away a little because you are encroaching on their comfort zone. Sometimes, we brush our bodies against other people unknowingly. This usually happens in narrow spaces when one person is trying to get past another, when queuing, in buses or in trains. It is better to wait for someone to walk through a narrow space rather than squeezing through and brushing against them.

Personal space in a crowd may seem like an oxymoron. But believe me, it's possible. When on a busy footpath or shopping at the local supermarket, keep moving. Don't stop in your tracks to take a phone call or suddenly turn around. And if you're a tourist, step to the side to take a picture of a tall building, a site or monument so that it does not hinder someone's line of vision.

> If you don't maintain regular eye contact in a conversation, it can be interpreted as discomfort, evasiveness, lack of confidence or boredom.

Finally, watch your volume. When talking on your cell phone, give yourself a buffer of at least 10 feet to conduct a semiprivate call without annoying others. If you must make or take a call when in a crowd, keep it as short and low as possible. I have passed several people, on the road or been around them at the train station or the airport, who conduct their personal business loudly on a call. In the right hands, a mobile phone can be a powerful and useful tool. Unfortunately, people using cell phones often erroneously think they are creating a bubble of personal space within the public domain. Within that bubble, people feel they can act as they would at home – complete with using inappropriate language and subject matter they would otherwise whisper in private. I understand that sometimes you may not realize you are being loud or are caught up in the moment. But take a moment to look around you. If you are disturbing people around you, someone is likely to make their displeasure known by their facial expressions. Watch out for those cues and modify your volume level.

> **Always remember...**
>
> Be aware of your surroundings and avoid being the annoying space stealer.
> The moment you step out of home, you are in a public place. So be mindful of others and act accordingly.

EYE CONTACT

Ralph Waldo Emerson said, "When the eyes say one thing and the tongue another, a practised man relies on the language of the first." Eye contact is probably the most important aspect of body language. Looking someone in the eye as you meet and talk with them shows you are paying attention. Good eye contact plays a large part in conveying our interest in others. Too much eye contact and you could be seen as aggressive; too little eye contact and you can be seen as uninterested. Direct eye contact shows openness and honesty. The correct way of eye contact is short, frequent glances.

Imagine an inverted triangle in your face with the base of it just above your eyes. The other two sides descend from it and come to a point between your nose and your lips. That's the suggested area to look at during business conversations. Socially, the point of the triangle drops to include the chin and neck areas.

But remember that there's a mere blink between gazing and staring. That is why you should break eye contact every five seconds or so. When breaking the eye contact, don't look down as this might indicate that you want the conversation to end. Instead, look up or to the side as if you are remembering something. If you don't maintain regular eye contact in a conversation, it can be interpreted as discomfort, evasiveness, lack of confidence or boredom. When you stare longer, it can be construed as being too direct, dominant and makes the other person uncomfortable. It's okay to glance away occasionally as long as your gaze returns quickly to the other person. At no point should you look over the person's shoulders as it shows you are seeking out someone more interesting to talk with.

Always remember...

Break eye contact every five seconds so you don't end up staring at the person.

Too much eye contact could be seen as aggressive and too little as disinterest. Strike a balance between the two.

POSTURE

A picture paints a thousand words and the same can be said about gestures. We subconsciously give away hints about our true feelings, through our movements and gestures. The way we move and carry ourselves communicates a wealth of information to the world.

Researchers at Harvard Business School conducted a formidable study. They had participants come into a lab and split them up into two groups. In one group, they had them project correct body language – these are expansive poses, great posture poses for five minutes. In the other group, they had them do defeated body language poses – contracted, tightly held arms and legs and low hanging heads also for five minutes. They then had these groups go into mock interviews where they had to deliver a speech to evaluators and answer questions. These were videotaped and rated for overall performance, the ability to be hired and for presentation quality. Not surprisingly, the group that stood in the power poses were rated higher for their speech and were more likely to be hired. Just standing in successful body language poses for five minutes before an interview affected the outcome of the interview.

Crossing your arms in front of you, especially when you are talking business, is a no-no. When you show your hands, it means you are an open, confident person. If you are sitting, your hands should either be loose in front of you or on the sides where they are visible. Fidgeting represents nervous, anxious energy. If you are fidgeting at an interview, it reduces your chances of getting the job. You may fidget because of boredom or habit, but that's not how people perceive it. Always curb the desire to fidget.

The correct way to stand is by periodically shifting your weight from leg to leg. That way, you look confident and comfortable. Extremely tall people, especially women in India, tend to slump because they are ashamed of their height. Never do that. Be proud of what you have. So many women desire your statuesque height.

How you sit is also very important. First, never tap your feet or repeatedly jiggle your leg up and down. This can be perceived as nervousness or boredom on your part. Women should keep their knees together when seated, preferably with their ankles crossed and men should avoid sitting with their legs excessively wide apart.

WHEN YOU GO FOR A JOB INTERVIEW

What you say at an interview and meeting, and how you conduct yourself will decide if you get the job. Your qualifications obviously matter. But you've already passed that test if you've been called for an interview. You have to make sure you stand out by conducting yourself in an exemplary manner at the interview.

It begins by arriving dressed appropriately. Depending on the position you are interviewing for, it would do good for men to dress in a full suit or a full-sleeved shirt, and a tie, with clean socks and polished shoes. Women should be smartly attired in a trouser suit, skirt and shirt, or a crisp salwar kameez/sari, making sure that nothing about the outfit is provocative in terms of hemline, neckline, transparency, etc. Lace, frills and ruffles are also not recommended for interviews. Keep your jewelry restricted to small pearl earrings and an unobtrusive watch. Anything more would be a distraction. Wear smart, comfortable shoes (with perhaps a two-inch heel for graceful carriage) meant for work wear and match it with the general colour range of your attire.

Next, arrive at least ten minutes early. Account for traffic on the way and other obstacles. If you have been called at 10 am, make sure you are there and have announced your arrival by 9.45 am. This shows you are serious about the interview and are respectful of the time they have taken out of their busy schedule to meet you.

Do your homework about the company and the global trends and developments in the area of your work. Walking into an interview blindly demonstrates lack of initiative. A friend's daughter went for an interview to a fashion website last year. While she knew about the website because it is quite famous, she did not know about the

> Never slouch while sitting, especially when you are meeting someone for professional reasons.

other things the company did, except for the profile that she was interested in. So when they started asking her questions about those other aspects, she was dumbstruck and made a fool of herself there. Until she proves her credentials in her field, I am afraid that company will never even consider giving her a second chance at an interview. I hope you never put yourself in that position.

Begin your interview by politely handing your business card to the others in the meeting. I understand that it is not always possible to directly offer your card from hand-to-hand – that may also look like you're trying too hard to make yourself known – you can place your card in front of their notebook. This shows you are professional, but it also helps others remember your name in the meeting. Similarly, accept the business card of whomever is offering you one in the room with both hands. After looking at it, place the card on the table right above your notebook, so you can glance at it during the meeting. Make sure you remember to take the card with you at the end of the meeting. All the rules discussed in the topic above on business cards apply here as well.

Next up, body language. Ask any employer. They will tell you they are always looking at your body language to gauge what kind of employee you will turn out to be. Sit up straight. You may think that a relaxed pose will show you are confident, but instead, it shows a lack of respect or interest. Don't sit with both hands on your lap beneath the table – you will look like a nervous child. Rest an arm on the arm of your chair or on the table. Make eye contact. Do not fidget in your chair, cross your legs, wring your hands, and try not to make too many hand gestures. Hold a pen if that helps you control your nervousness.

> Do not speak about your previous employers in a negative light no matter what the circumstances may have been. This will surely put a shadow of doubt on your ability to be professional and loyal.

I should not have to say this, but since I have observed many people do it, it deserves a mention. Never slouch while sitting, especially when you are meeting someone for professional reasons. A friend's son is one of those millennial kids who started and now runs a successful tech company. The office environment of such companies is very casual. He met a 22-year-old for an interview in his office. The interviewee was casually dressed, which was okay for that job profile. But he took casual a bit too far when he didn't sit up straight while answering questions from a potential employer. According to my friend's son, he was halfway down the chair with one ankle resting on the knee of the other leg. "Yes, we're not a company that promotes a formal atmosphere. But even for that, I felt that the interviewee seemed as if he wasn't taking the job seriously. This is someone I am probably going to pay plenty of money. I'm definitely not going to give it to someone who doesn't even know how to sit properly." That's what he told me when I met him a few months ago. So let this be a cautionary tale for everyone. You are being judged even when you think you are not. And you owe it to yourself to always be on your best behaviour.

After you shake hands, stand behind a chair until you are invited to sit down. Ease yourself into the chair, sit upright, place your hands in front of you and speak confidently to everyone present in the room, maintaining eye contact along the way. When you take your seat, do not place your personal items on the table – no cell phones, handbags, briefcases or water bottles. All these things should be placed next to your feet or on a chair beside you. The only things you can place on the table is your portfolio or folder.

Remember to turn off or mute your cell phone before you enter the room. If you have forgotten and it rings during the interview, do not look at the screen and do not answer it to explain that you cannot talk at that moment. Reach for it in your bag, disconnect the call immediately and turn the phone off. Don't forget to apologize to the interviewer.

Carry a neat, clean, unfolded copy of your updated resume and present it only if asked. Make sure it reflects details that are accurate and true. Do not make false claims, as they are bound to catch up with you at some time. When asked to introduce yourself, list details chronologically and keep it within the limits relevant to your professional graph. It is not necessary to cite the reasons for exiting previous employments unless asked.

Do not speak about your previous employers in a negative light no matter what the circumstances may have been. This will surely put a shadow of doubt on your ability to be professional and loyal. Diplomatically circumvent such situations citing growth and new associations for new employment. Do not ramble on and keep responses focused. Avoid being cocky and maintain a humble disposition when talking about your achievements, but do speak about them at the appropriate juncture of the interview.

Of course, feel free to ask questions pertinent to your role and growth within the organization because that's where you're going to be hopefully spending the next few years. But please don't ask frivolous questions, such as their break timings or dress code.

When the interview is over, shake hands with everyone in the room and leave the room with a confident stride. It would be nice to send a thank you note a few hours later if you are still interested in the job.

Always remember...

Carry a neat, updated resume and talk about your achievements.
Turn off your cell phone or put it on the vibrate mode.
Don't slouch and smile while answering every question.
Don't gossip about your previous employer.

HOW TO WRITE A RÉSUMÉ

Your résumé is a concise work history, list of accomplishments, and education that you present to a potential employer. Writing a resume takes time and attention to detail. The way you lay out your résumé is really a matter of preference; in fact, there are hundreds of sample résumés online that you have to replicate, but keep in mind that you want it to be as easy to read as possible, so leave plenty of white space.

Usually, you start with your contact information at the top. Of course, make sure all your contact information is correct. Your contact information is usually followed by a short description of your qualifications or skills that can be applied to the position you are seeking. That is usually followed by your work history, your education and achievements.

Choose the right font: You want your résumé to stand out, but for the right reasons, which begins the moment someone looks at it.

Your résumé is a representation of your professional avatar. It is not a space for artistic expression, which means you cannot ever use casual fonts. Do not ever use Comic Sans. You get about 10 to 20 seconds to make a first impression with your résumé, so make it count. If you have used an unprofessional font, no one is going to take it, and you, seriously. Most professionals use serif fonts, like Times New Roman, because they are perceived as being reliable, authoritative and traditional. Go with those.

Statement: Here's where you tell the employer what you would like to do. Whatever the type of position you are seeking, make sure it's clear. Also, include experience and skills you have attained in your past work to show how you qualify. For instance, if you are looking for a sales management position, mention how you will use your skills and experience in motivating staff, generating loyal customers, and project management to achieve and exceed the company's sales projections.

Job history: Starting with your most recent position, list the jobs you have had in descending order. Make sure you list the title and the duration and dates, you were employed at the company. Under each job, describe what your role was. Use point form sentences or bullets, and keep the phrases to the point. The same goes for mentioning your education too.

References: Write these on a separate page and don't give names of friends and relatives as references.

AND, ALWAYS SMILE

A smile has power that we are probably not even aware of. Smiling indicates happiness and a friendly attitude. Smiling indicates we want to communicate with someone and shows interest. You can literally never go wrong with a smile. Make that your best feature.

Learning to use and discern body language helps you become a better communicator. By understanding body language more effectively, we can decrease our chances of being misunderstood, causing conflicts and increase our chances of maintaining our friendships, hiring and be hired ourselves.

2

LANGUAGE

"I was raised right — I talk about people behind their backs. It's called manners."

— Kathy Griffin, comedian

know a gentleman. To say that he is rich would be an understatement. I went to listen to one of his speeches. Everyone was eager to hear what he had to say. He walked towards the microphone and before he could say a single word, he burped. Imagine how disgusting it would be to hear a burp. Now imagine hearing that sound loudly coming through a microphone. It was so repulsive. Here is a man who has access to the best things in life. He is a well-known philanthropist. Many people look up to him as an inspiration and role model. That's why so many of us went to hear him speak. But for us – the people present there – he will always be remembered as the man who burped so loudly that we wanted to chop our ears off.

I understand that I have begun this chapter on an extremely gross note. But this is a prime example of how not to behave in public. On a similar note, a close friend of mine has a habit of belching loudly. And according to her we shouldn't pay too much attention to it because she belches only in the presence of us, her close friends. We laugh it off because we have known her most of our lives. But because it's a habit, she once belched loudly when there were other guests around. It was embarrassing for her as well as the others. This is why it is important to practise manners at home. If you don't do something within the confines of your home, you will never do it outside. My friend has now learnt her lesson and after that incident, she swore to never belch in public. A large part of etiquette is knowing what to say and what not to say to someone you are talking to. People will never forget a wrong word spoken at the wrong time. And you have to live with the knowledge of that faux pas forever. So why not avoid putting your foot in your mouth in the first place?

HOW TO HAVE A CONVERSATION

Talking is an important form of communication. Every time you open your mouth, you reveal something about yourself, not just in what you say, but how you say it too. That's why it's important to know what to speak when and to whom.

Arm yourself with topics: How do you strike up a conversation with someone you don't know at all, or at least not well enough? On your way, think of three topics to talk about. It makes your life so much simpler. If you don't know the people you will be conversing with, think about the things that will probably interest them. For example, ask them about the unique aspects of their location ('I saw an interesting statue on the way here. Do you know the story behind it?') Or read up on the company they work for ('I hear you will be expanding into China soon. Will that affect you?') But if you're going to a party and don't know people there very well, ask the host for their names and do some homework. Maybe, they are avid cricket fans or are foodies. These topics will warm both of you up for better and more insightful conversations. To draw out a conversation, never ask a question for which there is a monosyllabic answer. Questions like 'How was your day?' or 'Did you like the movie?' will not serve your purpose. Instead, 'What's your opinion on the latest Batman movie?' will get the person talking. There's no way they can give a yes or no answer if you frame your question correctly.

> Avoid conversational narcissism. No matter how much you know about a particular topic that's being discussed, always remember that your goal is to have a comfortable conversation. Let the other person talk too.

Use their name: Always use people's names when you are addressing them. 'That's an interesting point, Mahesh.' 'So when did you arrive, Namrata?' People always like that, especially in the business world. Keep using their names a few times in the conversation. When you use someone's name, it shows that you are interested in hearing what they have to say, that their opinion matters to you. Of course, make an effort to remember their names.

Listen more than you talk: Ironically enough, the key to the art of conversation is not in the talking, but in the listening. Avoid conversational narcissism. No matter how much you know about a particular topic that's being discussed, always remember that your goal is to have a comfortable conversation. Let the other person talk too. I had read a story, years ago, in *Reader's Digest*, where a woman was complaining to her friend about her in-laws. And after she was done, she said, "Thank you for not sharing your in-laws' story." Her friend understood that at that time, her job was to listen and not contribute with similar experiences of her own. That is why you should resist the temptation to always take the spotlight. Ask the other person interesting and thoughtful questions. One of the most common starters to a conversation is asking about their work. But don't ask what someone does and leave it at that. Ask them what the hardest part of their job is, how the future of their profession looks. Then ask follow-up questions. This again shows you are interested and giving them the importance that they deserve. Nod your head, and add 'hmms' and 'uh-huhs' at appropriate moments. Don't let your eyes wander; that's extremely insulting. Also don't interrupt them. Wait for a break in a sentence and then talk. Be interesting when you are contributing too. However, we all know that sometimes some people are just too boring and that it is impossible to talk to them for a longer amount of time. That's why I believe that you should talk to someone for a minimum of two minutes. If they continue to bore you after that, politely make your excuses – 'I need to get a drink' or 'I have to answer a call' – and step away with a little white lie saying, "It was lovely talking to you."

Take your turn: Yes, it's an interesting discussion and you want to have your say. But there's no need to butt into a conversation, especially when someone else is speaking. Start by joining the group, get a feel of what is being said by listening in and when there's a break, offer your take on the topic under discussion. Similarly, if you notice that you have spoken for a few minutes without any questions or comments from other people, it is likely that you are being a conversation hog. Cede the floor to someone else. On the same note, it's always nice to talk to someone who looks alone in a room full of people. Maybe they are awkward; maybe they are feeling out of place. A little empathy goes a long way.

Be knowledgeable: It's very important for you to be updated with what's happening around the world. You cannot be an interesting conversationalist if you don't have knowledge. Years ago, I remember talking with friends about an India-West Indies cricket match that had taken place the day before. We were analysing the match when one of them said, "And did you see how Lara bowled? Wasn't he wonderful?" In hindsight, we should not have done that but we all burst out laughing. She was talking about the batsman Brian Lara who has probably bowled only a few overs in his cricketing career. And he had definitely not bowled in that match. If my friend had done a bit of homework, she wouldn't have made such a big faux pas. That's why it's always helpful to at least read the headlines if you don't have time to go through the whole newspaper. That way you will be an interesting contributor to any conversation without looking like a fool.

Think before you speak: I cannot reiterate this enough. Thinking before speaking is a challenge for many people. Speaking without thinking can get you in trouble and hurt you and the people you are interacting with. Relationships can suffer or end and careers get stalled because people don't filter their thoughts. Don't let that happen to you.

> **Always remember...**
> Be aware of what's happening around you, in the world, so you always have something interesting to talk about.
> Use people's names while talking to them, it provides a personal touch.
> People love talking about themselves, so ask them questions to keep the conversation flowing.
> Have a mental filter.

THINGS TO NEVER TALK ABOUT

There are certain things we just don't talk about, especially when it's a stranger. Remember how annoyed you got when acquaintance after acquaintance asked you when you were getting married? First, it's none of their business, and second, it's just plain rude. Similarly, asking someone about their personal life, political leaning, sexual orientation, religious beliefs, age, weight, financial condition and illnesses is never a good idea. They can believe whatever they want to about these things; you don't get an opinion on it.

The first thing women tend to do when they meet someone is talk about their weight. 'You've lost so much weight,' or 'What have you been eating?' are common things we hear. Most people never stop to consider the consequences of their statements. They may believe they are saying something harmless, but what if it's not? Why take a chance? It's best to just say, "You look lovely tonight" and leave it at that. This incident happened years ago when I was a part of the aviation industry. My friend and I had gone to a supermarket abroad. She was a big person and had a big belly. As we approached the cash counter, one of the staff told her that there was a separate checkout counter for pregnant women. My friend was fuming and was highly offended. She gave the person a dirty look, clarified that she wasn't pregnant and stormed out of the store. "How dare they assume something when they know nothing about me?" she said later. I understand that the staff was only trying to be helpful and doing their jobs. But you have to use your common sense too and see each situation and person individually. Many people encounter something similar while travelling by public transport. We are taught to offer our seat to old people, women with children as well as pregnant women. We all want to help, but in trying to be noble, we can mistake a plump woman for a pregnant one and risk offending them. It's a better idea to just offer your seat without bringing up the pregnancy. They will accept or refuse your offer depending on whether they need to sit or not. It's best to not assume.

Weight is, and I fear will always be, a touchy topic. I have concluded that it is one of the first things two women will talk about at a party. Whether someone has gained weight or lost it, it's none of your business. Don't make the other person uncomfortable by asking questions they may not want to answer. I will explain this with an example. We all believe that only overweight people are sensitive about it, so most people don't bring that up in a conversation with them. But very thin people are conscious about their weight too. Telling a thin person to eat a lot so that they gain weight is such a common conversation. A friend of my friend is a thin person – thin enough for people to notice. Once, years ago, when they were just acquaintances, my friend commented on how she never had to worry about weight because she was so thin. She meant that as a compliment and then moved on to another topic. She did not think twice about that statement she made until another friend pointed it out to her. "Did you look at her face when

> When you are in a group, don't crack inside jokes. Keeping people out of the conversation is extremely insulting.

you made that weight-loss statement? Her face fell instantly." My friend was so shocked that she had failed to notice her reaction. It had never occurred to her that her low weight could be a sensitive topic. Her friend has been underweight all her life and had been subjected to comments from 'well-meaning' friends and relatives for years. That incident really opened my friend's eyes and she resolved to think before she spoke and not assume anything. My daughter, too, has been on the receiving end of such comments all her life. She's naturally a thin person and I have had so many people ask me for years if I feed her properly. My daughter is very healthy and I, too, have reiterated that her body is fine the way it is. But the effect of hearing hurtful comments all her life means that she also sometimes thinks she should eat more than she can because that will help her gain weight.

Hurtful comments are not just about weight. People, especially women, are subjected to all sorts of comments regarding their appearance. Once at a get-together, I was chatting with a few women in a group and one of them told the other, "I know a wonderful dermatologist. She will remove the mole on your face easily and you'll look so beautiful." The other woman was taken aback and replied saying that she loved her mole. Now that is an uncomfortable situation. The first woman meant well, but sometimes we don't realize what comes out of our mouths. Refrain from giving advice or being the Good Samaritan when it can backfire.

I saw a great quote on Facebook once. It goes, 'You shouldn't point out things about people's appearances if they can't fix it in ten seconds.' Truer words have not been spoken. The world would be a much nicer and respectful place if all of us made this our mantra.

Also, never bitch about anyone or their family members, keep conversations light, and remember that jokes are fine as long as they are not offensive. Always take the person's lead before you talk about a sensitive topic. I have a friend who is very loving and only means well. But every time I order dessert, she takes a bone of chicken and puts it next to the dessert and says, "Now let's see you eat it." While I'm not a vegetarian, it's still rude to put her half-eaten food on my plate. I know that she's doing me a favour by making sure I don't consume more sugar than I should, but maybe I want a bite of something sweet. That's not a crime. I would love to have her hourglass figure, but that's not the way for her to get me one.

When you are in a group, don't crack inside jokes. Keeping people out of the conversation is extremely insulting. I have also observed many people speaking in their mother tongue in a group while talking to just one person. That is just not done. Imagine if someone did that in your presence. Wouldn't you feel out of place and think that they were talking about you? So why would you do that to someone else?

> **Always remember...**
>
> Do not talk about someone's weight, religion or political inclination.
> Talk in such a manner that you include everyone in the conversation.
> Do not talk badly about someone who is not present. It speaks more about you than them.

HOW TO START A CONVERSATION

You are at a party or a conference or at someone's home for dinner. It may be someone who is a good customer or investor for your company, or someone you simply like the looks of. You struggle for the right thing to say that would get both of you talking, but before you can come up with anything good, the person has moved on or gotten involved in a different conversation and the moment has passed. It's amazing how we are engulfed with communication from all ends – the media, children, our own thirst to connect with those around us – and yet there are times when we are quite stumped for conversation. If this has happened to you, it need not ever happen again. You can gracefully start a conversation with absolutely anyone, anytime. There's only one secret: say something the person will be happy to hear. With these conversation starters, you can navigate any social situation.

WHEN YOUR SPOUSE BRINGS A COLLEAGUE HOME

Your spouse brings home a colleague for the first time and because you are a good host, you have to put your guest at ease. Welcome them and ask if you can offer them any refreshments. Once you have food and drinks in your hands, you can talk to them about their family – their parents, their own family. In case your guest is unmarried, do not construe this as an invitation to matchmake. It is also not polite to ask about the reason for their single status. Do they have children? How old are they? Do they go to school? Which one? This will help create connecting questions that may lead to talking about the development of the education system in our country, on which both of you may exchange personal views, and move on to a general discussion about education.

What not to say

Don't ask personal questions about salary or whether or they are satisfied with the current company and position.

Do not monopolize the conversation. After a few niceties, excuse yourself and allow your spouse to take over. They will probably have more common things to talk about.

AT A SCHOOL FUNCTION

At any cultural or academic function at your child's school, other parents surround you. Your most bankable conversation opener is clearly the class, subjects and progress of your children. Do keep the conversation light and chat about how education in India has evolved, educational options available today (home schooling, etc.), academic and professional aspirations of your respective children, what colleges they are considering and new extracurricular activities and recreation for children, among others.

What not to say

Don't be overly competitive and nosey about the exact marks or grades of the other children. Congratulate them if their child wins an award or competition.

MEETING PROSPECTIVE SPOUSES OF RELATIVES

Say your niece or nephew brings home their spouse or fiancé/eé for the first time to meet you. You have the responsibility of making the new entrant into your family feel welcome. Take the lead and extend your hospitality.

You can chat about...

Where and how the couple met. Talk about where your spouse and you met, or how the niece/nephew's parents met and share anecdotes about their and your courting.

Food likes and dislikes, or allergies. Talk about your family's eating habits and suggest that they try out dishes that your family members are great at, i.e. your mother's biryani or sister's steak.

Ask whether they like to cook. Suggest a potluck dinner where you can sample their cooking without pressurising them to cook the entire meal.

Share anecdotes of your nephew or niece, but steer away from the sensitive ones. If you have them at hand, show them baby photographs of the niece or nephew. That should have you sail through the entire evening and more.

What not to say

Never bitch about any family members, even if you think you are giving them advice. There will be enough time for that later.

AT A WEDDING

At an acquaintance's wedding, you are likely to be surrounded by people you have never met before, but have to make conversation with. Keep it simple and allow them to do the talking:

Ask them how they know the wedding hosts, and respond with how you know them.

Comment positively on the ceremony and the decorations.

If they are married, encourage them to talk about their own wedding ceremony.

Talk about any unusual wedding themes you might have witnessed.

What not to say

In all situations, it remains important that you do not indulge in negativity. You don't want your first impression to be of a person who gossips.

Do keep the conversation light and slip in jokes, as long as they are not personal or offensive.

While eating, refrain from talking about illness and their gory symptoms. If someone else begins talking about the matter, sympathize and quickly turn the conversation to something less unappetising.

Don't offer information about how many calories the dessert contains just as the other person is piling it on their plate.

WHEN YOU ARE IN A FORMAL SETTING

You have to be careful about what you say at work too. You are constantly being appraised and you always have to be on your best behaviour. A workplace demands the highest standards from you and you have to strive constantly to match them. This is especially true when you are working in the service sector. You are a representative of your

> A workplace demands the highest standards from you and you have to strive constantly to match them.

company. I was training the staff of a very high-end jewelry store on how to behave with customers. The salesgirls shared an incident that's a good example of the opposite of exemplary customer service. One day, a gentleman walked in, who looked nothing like the customers they usually had. He was wearing *chappals*, had a big turban and they said he looked like a vegetable vendor. Thinking of him as unimportant, they did not give him any attention. One of the girls happened to speak with him by walking past him and he took out his turban, which was full of cash, and said he wanted to buy a jewelry set for his daughter. The one huge mistake they made was that they judged someone based on their appearance. If you are in the sales business, you have to treat everyone as a potential buyer. It is your duty as a salesperson to extend that courtesy to everyone that you meet, regardless of what you think of them.

I have another example of workplace behaviour that is just unacceptable. I went to Hong Kong recently and visited a store in a mall. I was just browsing, but the woman at the counter had a very bad attitude. As a buyer, I had the right to be there and check out what the store had to offer. But nothing appealed to me, and I was exiting the store when the woman shouted at me saying, "Don't waste my time next time." Normally, I would have just walked away. But I turned around and told her, "You're in the wrong profession. It is your duty to show me the stuff in your store, whether I want to buy it or not." But she didn't even understand what I was trying to tell her. She continued to shout at me. This is the absolute wrong attitude. If you have chosen a job in the sales industry, you have to be polite. Yes, you will get angry towards a customer, but that doesn't mean you do anything about it. The only thing you can do is smile and learn to let it go.

WHEN YOU ARE THE BOSS

Recently, I was left cringing when a close associate of mine rudely shouted and insulted his subordinate for a minor slip, which actually was no fault of his. The fact that I cringe often can in no way reduce the magnitude of the offence or the boorish display of behaviour. Unfortunately, such incidents are more the rule than the exception. And it is the informed, educated and aware who are the worst perpetrators. Whatever happened to the fine art of living courteously with malice towards none?

That subordinate staff or menial labour exists outside the periphery of our insular lives is more a matter of fact than fiction. The truth is that there is a crying need for reforms concerning boss-subordinate relationships. It's a complex issue and we are light years away from achieving dignity for labour. Moreover, external forces influence our behaviour largely.

There is no excuse for using and abusing any person. Being authoritative is necessary, but power affords a tremendous high and it would be futile not to keep your feet firmly planted on the ground. The unpopular, mean and nasty bully never ever wins staff loyalty. It does not require a great analytical mind to figure out that a comfortable, congenial working atmosphere is not only the ideal working condition, but improves productivity as well.

People in authority need to lead by example and the rest will follow suit. Respect, once given, is always returned a thousandfold; even more so if you take care to ensure a fair and just company policy.

- Induction for subordinate staff should include office etiquette. I would recommend that the management promote staff welfare by advocating basic human kindness and consideration.

- Pleasantly acknowledge when a member of your staff greets you. Initiate a greeting if none is forthcoming.

- Keep your staff happy – if you have to be a taskmaster, at least be a kind one. Give them some time off at regular intervals and reward their effort. Remember there is pleasure in giving as well as receiving.

- Never fly off the handle. Hollering and screaming at someone who cannot do the same in return is pathetic behaviour.

- Convey all information and instructions calmly but firmly without using foul language.

- Get to know your staff. Inquire about their families. Send a personal greeting on birthdays and wedding anniversaries.

- Treat others as you would have them treat you.

DEALING WITH WORK-SHIRKING SUBORDINATES

It's a misconception that 'team spirit' requires you to take the fall. A group is called a team only when each member pulls his or her own weight. An occasional problem does however, warrant concern from an exacting boss. You are doing him a disservice by assisting his development into a con artist. Your leadership qualities are under the scanner here as well. In my opinion, since the person concerned has the capabilities, it would be to your credit if you got him to pull his weight. Besides, your team's productivity is being seriously compromised with all this pent up emotion and resentment.

Here's what you should do:

- Stand up for your rights. Don't give him the pleasure of scoring a home run again. Gently but firmly tell him that you are all on to his tricks and that you will blow his cover should he try a repeat performance.

- Sit him down and have a heart-to-heart – in private, of course. Apprise him of the situation caused by his selfish attitude. Simultaneously highlight his skills, his talent and his competence that are presently being underutilized and overshadowed.

- Keep your manner firm but pleasant and avoid being confrontational or derogatory.

- Open his eyes to the fact that a reputation is slow to build but quick to ruin. And that a good reputation is vital to career growth.

- Give him a target and a time limit for his reformation. He should be aware that you will blow the whistle on his tricks.

- Be discriminatory, sensitive and intuitive to determine if he is a terminal, psychological or pathological case. Should this be the case, it is your duty to inform the authorities immediately.

- Be discreet. Let it not be the hot topic of discussion on coffee breaks. On the flip side, you would be harming your own career if you let the problem get the better of you. Remaining silent is, by the way, being a tacit accomplice.

What do you do when a colleague, senior or peer has bad breath, smelly feet or body odour?

I am asked this question quite frequently. It's very difficult working in close proximity, but one doesn't want to offend them either. Here again, a person's tact and diplomacy is under the scanner, but I do understand your dilemma. Foul odours can make you gag, rendering interaction almost impossible. But I want to dispel any notion that the person concerned is unhygienic. Toxins in the human body vary from person to person and hyperactive toxins emit a bad odour vitiating the atmosphere. Most often, the person is either unaware or in denial. You will need to handle the problem with kid gloves, in the gentlest possible way. Smelling good yourself and being impeccably groomed often encourages an aspirational quality. Pop mints in your mouth and offer some to those around, including your friend or colleague. This will effectively take care of the bad breath. If you enjoy a close rapport with the person, bring to his or her awareness the problem. Out of earshot of the rest, suggest a good deodorant, a dentist or a chiropodist – should a recommendation be called for. Finally, be a confidante, encouraging, and understanding. This problem can be devastating and isolating at times.

> ## Always remember...
>
> Be polite to everyone in office – from your boss to the office boy.
>
> Treat your subordinates the way you want to be treated – with respect. Taking advantage of your position only shows you in a bad light.
>
> But that does not mean you let your subordinates take you for granted. If he or she is not performing the way they should, it's part of your job to pull them up and ask them to change the way they work.

PHONE ETIQUETTE

A few months ago, I received a 'wrong number' call. I answered the phone and was greeted by a very rude, "Who's this?" The woman got angry when I said, "No, who is THIS?" I was not wrong to ask that because she is the one who had called me. Then she asked if this was the so-and-so residence. When I politely told her that she must have dialled the wrong number, she again very angrily demanded, "What number is this, anyway?"

Talking with someone on the phone effectively is truly an art form. When you are talking online, you have the time to devise a great answer and think about what you are going to speak about before you press the Enter key. And when you are talking to someone in person, you can use your facial expressions and body language to get your point across better. But when you are talking on the phone, it's all about the tone of your voice and the way you speak to them. That's why the telephone is the worst means of communication and why having good manners on the phone is so important.

Telephone etiquette means being respectful to the person you are talking with, allowing that person time to speak and communicate clearly. Your voice must create a pleasant visual impression of you. Here are some points to keep in mind while conversing on the phone.

1. Always answer the phone within three rings. Identify yourself at the beginning of all calls. If you are at work, answer a telephone call by saying, "Good morning, [your name] speaking. How may I assist you?" You always identify yourself on the phone because calls get disconnected sometimes and you may need to call them back to continue the conversation. Then you can ask for the person you were talking to instead of having to explain the same thing to someone else.

2. Do not eat or chew gum while talking on the telephone.

3. Talking on a cell phone when you are driving can be as dangerous as driving drunk. If you must make or receive a call in the car, pull over. You will be doing yourself and everyone else on the road a huge favour.

4. Speak softly. Cell phones are normally much more sound sensitive than regular phones, so you don't need to yell to make yourself heard. And no amount of shouting will

improve a bad connection.

5. Be mindful of the tone of your voice. Do not sound aggressive or pushy. Your tone should convey authority and confidence. You may not be speaking in a rude manner, but if the tone of your voice is not correct, you will be misinterpreted.

6. Respect the personal space of others by taking your call away from people. Ideally, take your phone call into a private space. Avoid using your phone in a place where others cannot escape overhearing your conversation, like in an elevator or on public transit.

7. Do not carry on side conversations with other people around you while you have a call. The person on the telephone takes precedence over someone who happens to walk into your office or passes by while you are on the phone. If you must interrupt the conversation, say, "Please excuse me. I'll be right back." And when you return, say, "Thank you for holding." Similarly, answering a call while having a face-to-face conversation with another person is a no-no. By conducting a phone conversation in front of that person, you are insultingly them and indicating that they are not important enough to you. Should an emergency arise, politely excuse yourself. Explain that it's a phone call you have to answer or were expecting. Leave your present company and then answer the call.

8. Often, we get marketing calls where they want to talk to you about a promotional deal or offer. I know they can be very annoying, especially when you are in the middle of work. But understand that they're trying to do their job too. If you are not interested, just say that you are not, say thank you and end the call. If they still insist, you can disconnect the call because you have done your part by telling them you don't want to hear what they're saying. But there's no need to bark at telemarketers.

9. If you have a conference call, ensure you are there on time. Tell the person you are putting them on the speaker before you do so. Then introduce everyone present at the meeting.

10. Do not talk so loudly on the phone that you disturb the person sitting next to you. You have to be especially careful

while travelling on public transport. In our busy lives, everyone is always trying to claim a bit of personal and private space even in public. Respect that. No one should be subjected to the phone conversation you are having. Keep private matters private. It's embarrassing to be privy to cell phone conversations about your marital problems. And if you're using the phone for business, you could leak company-confidential information when talking in public.

11. Few things are more irritating than being put on hold as soon as your call has been picked up. And the worst thing is that this is a common occurrence. Remember the last time that happened to you? When you called customer service? And how maddening that was? That is why you shouldn't do that to someone else. But sometimes it is necessary to do put the caller on hold. The right way to do that is to answer the phone and ask them politely whether it is all right if you put them on hold for a few seconds. Wait for the person to respond. Only when they say yes, do you do it.

12. Turn your cell phone off or put it on silent mode during weddings, funerals, movies, live performances, sports events, business meetings, classes and dates, and in places of worship, restrooms, restaurants, libraries, museums and in doctor or dentist waiting rooms. It's extremely ill-mannered to do otherwise.

13. Be wary of novelty ring tones. Not everyone will appreciate hearing the latest tune every time you receive a call. Try using your phone's vibrate function instead of the ringer in public.

14. Finally, always return a call you have missed within 24 hours.

HANGING OUT WITH PEOPLE YOU DON'T LIKE

You may often find yourself in a situation where you are obliged to hang out with someone you don't particularly like. It could be someone from your partner's other circle of friends, for instance, or your husband's overly critical aunt. Either way, you cannot get out of meeting them every so often; and although their comments bother you, you'd ideally prefer to maintain a cordial relationship for the sake of propriety. However, it's human nature for your tolerance to falter. Do you set them straight once and for all? Or is it best to just ignore them? Is it okay to be mean in return? Or you don't want to lose your decorum?

Etiquette under pressure: It takes all types to make this world, and at some stage, you may be compelled to interact with a wisecracking person. It is admittedly an irresistible joy to maliciously retaliate to a snide remark aimed at you. But, no matter how tempting, I personally wouldn't stoop to that level. More often than not, envy and insecurity manifest itself in an inferiority complex, which is the root of such evil. Since you cannot avoid hanging out with this person, maintain a cordial attitude. A polite greeting will unnerve them and they will have no option but to be polite to you in return. Nastiness in the face of your civility will only make them look petty.

Keep your distance: Just because you are hanging out at the same place, whether it's a party or a wedding, doesn't mean you have to hang around that person. If talking to them is really going to bother you, keep some space between you, and keep yourself occupied with your friends. Also, don't start bad-mouthing them. The people around you are likely to pass on that, which will only cause more problems.

Keeping good humour: Curb that itch to bitch. Good etiquette is about being cool and collected with complete emotional control. Engaging in gentle sparring can be fun, provided you avoid the mudslinging. However, constant sparring and bickering will only isolate you from the people you like. When you are the target of malicious intent, change the subject, speaking softly, or just walk away. Sometimes, treating viciousness with good humour diffuses a situation and takes the wind out of their sails. Ignore the spiteful person and shift your focus to a friendly face. When communicating, it is always safe to address the group in general. Confrontational dialogue is asking for trouble.

> Curb that itch to bitch. Good etiquette is about being cool and collected with complete emotional control.

If the situation and the person become unbearable remember

that, you are an adult who can choose how to react. Take a deep breath and detach.

FIRST DAY AT WORK

The first day at work can be a nerve-wracking experience. But there are ways to keep a calm demeanour. Regardless of our confidence and competence, we all undergo some amount of nervousness and apprehension when starting a new job. Moreover, day one is literally just the beginning. If it's any consolation, let it be known that we are not alone in this nervousness; the people in the company that we will be part of will also experience this; after all, it will be their day one with you, too.

Keep a few points in mind and you will find yourself in a more secure space than you think.

- Make sure that you arrive at work at least 15 minutes ahead, as this will give you the chance to soak in your physical space and draw comfort from familiarity.

- Dress appropriately. Formal business wear is always better to don rather than casual wear. If the office dress code is casual, it is easier to remove the jacket and roll up your sleeves but if the dress code is formal and you have shown up in casual attire, where are you going to find a jacket to fit in!

- If you have been hired in a position that takes charge of a team, have the recruiting head set up a brief introductory meeting where you familiarize yourself with the people you will be working with.

- Exchange information that gives you insights on the beliefs, strengths and abilities of the individuals.

- Share in brief, your role and agenda and the goals you aim to set. The course to chart those goals can be left for discussion at a later stage. Orient the team with your preferred method of working so that they are able to deliver accordingly.

- If, however, you have been hired into a position that is part of a team that reports to a head, do some homework and prepare yourself with an agenda that you will follow.

- Discuss this agenda with your reporting head to see if it is in keeping with the team's way forward. Make sure that you take instructions on the working process, objectives and goals, both short-term and long-term.

- Meet with the Human Resource team, as this team will assist you in the way forward.

- While you may have a single person taking you through the organization, do not allow yourself to be manipulated by his or her choice of whom you would need to orient yourself with. Take the lead and meet people from whom you believe you will learn, gather information from or perhaps even need as a sounding board moving forward.

- Do not hesitate to request the relevant HR person to equip you with adequate support material and stationery that you will need to conduct your work. Make a list of the things that you will need and hand it over and organize yourself once you have received it.

- Find out if there are any rules to be followed towards, usage of the internet, facsimile, photocopy and scanning machines, international phone calls, business cards, conference rooms, cafeteria, office errand staff, conveyance, reimbursements, etc.

- Adopt a neutral attitude and refrain from giving ear to any gossip, falling into any factions or being judgmental.

- Be open to suggestions and recommendations by seniors and colleagues and refrain from being opinionated on every situation. Take time to soak in the professional and human culture of the organization before expressing an opinion or affecting decisions.

- Do not encourage personal visits or telephone calls from family or friends, especially on day one!

Always remember...

Talking on the phone while driving is a big, giant NO. You're putting your life as well as that of others at risk. No phone call is that important.

Don't be rude to telemarketers. It's their job to call you.

Speak softly, especially if you are in a public place.

DICTION

Pronunciation is vital to proper communication because the incorrect use of pronunciation can lead to misrepresentation of what you are trying to do. Pronunciation is definitely the biggest thing that people notice when you are speaking English. The English language is so confusing. So speaking correctly is very important, especially if you want to avoid misunderstandings.

The next time you are talking to someone, just see how he or she says the word 'very'. Nine out of ten times, people don't know how to pronounce Vs and Ws. An easy way to get it right is to bite your Vs and kiss your Ws. Practice saying, 'It was very wet on a windy evening in Venice.' I wish this were an audio book. I could tell you more easily how to do that. If you don't know how to bite the Vs and kiss the Ws, listen to a few clips on YouTube. They will help you well.

Another thing to remember is that you should never cover your mouth while talking. Many of us lip read even though we can hear the words. Avoiding too much gesticulation while talking is also a good idea. It just distracts from what you are saying.

> Avoiding too much gesticulation while talking is also a good idea. It just distracts from what you are saying.

Many people don't know how to pronounce so many common words. You pronounce the word 'the' as 'thee' when it precedes a word starting with a vowel. For example, it's always 'thee apple', 'thee elephant'. 'The' is pronounced the common way when the following word starts with a consonant. For example, 'the bus', 'the dog'. Make a conscious effort to reverse these issues by practising.

It's sad that people judge you based on how well you can speak English. You can, of course, choose not to care about how people perceive you, and be ready to accept harsh judgements and rejections based on that. Or you can relearn how to speak English. With a few changes and a little bit of effort, you can impress everyone with your speaking skills.

3

TRICKY SOCIAL SITUATIONS

"Etiquette is all human social behavior. If you are a hermit on a mountain, you don't have to worry about etiquette; if somebody comes up the mountain, then you've got a problem. It matters because we want to live in reasonably harmonious communities."

— Judith Martin, American author

No matter how wealthy, attractive or powerful you are, none of them will save you from the unflattering label of being rude or insensitive to others' feelings. While the practice of good manners has diminished with the rise of technology, a polite demeanour is still an attribute that everyone appreciates, whether it's in a business situation or a social one. This is true for us adults as well as children. So let me start at the beginning, with kids.

KIDS' ETIQUETTE

Years ago, I had conducted a workshop for children between the ages of eight and fourteen years. It was a day-long workshop where some of the parents sent their kids with the domestic help, while others had sent them alone. During the break, biscuits and soft drinks were served. One of the kids knocked her plate and the biscuits fell on the ground. She bent to pick them up, but another child came to her and said, "Don't touch that. The servants will do it. And let them eat it. We never eat off the ground." I was horrified to hear that. Where had she learnt that? Clearly from her family.

A friend of mine told me about an incident she witnessed. She was at Zurich airport waiting for her flight back home to India. Couples with kids surrounded her. There was a sculpture at the airport that could have passed off as a jungle gym for kids but where a clear 'do not touch' sign was put up. While the kids may have been too young to read, but the parents clearly could. In complete disregard for the rules, the kids started jumping all over the sculpture and playing catch. Watching them, another child too joined them. Soon, a security officer came there and told the kids to stay away from the piece of art. The children went back to their parents, but in a few minutes, they started playing there again. The parents did nothing to stop them, while the parents of the child who joined the playgroup last forbade him from going back. Why could some parents follow the rules, and the others not? Not only did they not adhere to the rules in the first place, they also did not correct their children, even when they knew better. What kind of adults are these going to become? Kids always follow by example. If they see you helping an older person, they will do the same. If you are an abusive, disrespectful person who does not care for the rules, I guarantee that's how the kids will be too someday.

Even two-year-olds can learn to say 'please' and 'thank you.' Even though they don't yet understand the social graciousness of these words, your toddler learns that 'please' is how you get what you want and 'thank you' is how you end an interaction. At least you have planted these social niceties into your child's vocabulary; later your child will use them with the understanding that they make others feel good about helping you. When you ask your child to give you something, start the sentence with 'please' and end it with 'thank you.' Even before your child understands the meaning of these words, they learn they are important because mummy and daddy use them a lot.

On a similar note, there's an affluent family I know and they have a little boy who is in preschool. We were meeting them in someone's home and for some reason he kept hurling abuses at everyone. And the parents, instead of telling him to mind himself, laughed it off, saying, "How cute." I was shocked and told his mother that he was not behaving

> Very rarely will someone notice if your child is polite, but they will always notice if your kids are demanding or rude.

properly at all. But she had her excuses ready. She blamed the child's busy father and that he would be taught manners anyway when he would start going to school. This sends out a wrong message to the child that it's okay to behave badly.

There is no perfect way of raising children. If there were, all parents would buy the same book and raise their kids. We do our best as parents. Reprimanding them, how much to give in to them, encouraging them, all these things are just trial and error. I really thought I was being a good parent then, but when I look back, I realize that I was very protective of my daughter. I crippled my child's growth. I would not even send her in the lift alone with the watchman even when she was much older and could be trusted to take care of herself. Today, she asks me before making most decisions and she is dependant.

The basics of good values and manners have to be imbibed in them repeatedly. We have to do our best to make them good, compassionate, thoughtful human beings. One thing parents should avoid is fight in front of the kids. The other problems that arise from that situation aside, kids grow up thinking that that is normal. They believe it's okay to raise your voice and abuse someone else in the presence of others. They may grow up to behave badly in public – never mind who's watching. Very rarely will someone notice if your child is polite, but they will always notice if your kids are demanding or rude.

As a parent, you want to provide guidance about basic etiquette to your children as they grow, as well as teach them how to treat others respectfully. Basic etiquette includes table manners, phone etiquette, greeting others and thanking people for gifts. One rule I established a long time ago is no cell phones on the table when we have food. That is family time and it is very disrespectful to have someone on the phone. It shows that what's in the phone is more important than the person sitting in front of them.

Be polite to your staff. Kids should learn that just because someone works for you, it doesn't give you the right to treat them badly. Everyone is equal and should be treated equally. If the parents of that girl in that workshop of mine years ago had done the same, she wouldn't have thought that servants can be treated in a shabby manner.

If a child has behaved badly in front of others, how do you reprimand them? The best way to deal with that is to be firm and explain to them why their behaviour is wrong. Then take away a privilege of theirs. That way kids will understand that there are consequences to their bad behaviour and because they were insensitive to the needs of others, there is a punishment.

Most parents reprimand their kids when they behave badly, but forget to praise them when they act right. But why should I praise something that they should be doing in the first place, anyway? You do that so they know they have done something right. They will remember how they felt when you praised them and to replicate that feeling, they will behave well repeatedly. That's a win-win for everyone, isn't it?

MANNERS AT THE DINING TABLE

George Washington was just about 16 (sometime around 1744) when he transcribed *Rules of Civility & Decent Behaviour In Company and Conversation*. Funny how many of the 110 rules still apply, like 'think before you speak' or 'gaze not on the marks or blemishes of others and ask not how they came'.

Tell your kids that table manners are more than about proper eating; it's about being kind and considerate of others. Tell them although you know that they are smart and nice, other people may judge them on how they behave. Whether in a restaurant or in a house, here are some basic table manners:

- Don't stuff your mouth full of food; it looks gross, and you could choke.
- Chew with your mouth closed and don't talk with your mouth full. No one wants to see food being chewed or hear it being chomped on.
- Eat with a fork unless the food is meant to be eaten with fingers.
- Don't make rude comments about the food being served. It will hurt someone's feelings.
- Always say 'thank you' when served something. It shows appreciation.
- Don't gobble. Someone took a long time to prepare the food,

enjoy it slowly.

- When eating rolls, break off a piece of bread before buttering it. Eating a whole piece of bread looks tacky.

- Don't reach over someone's plate for something; ask for the item to be passed to you.

- Don't pick anything out of your teeth. Use a napkin to dab your mouth (which should be on your lap when not in use). But don't wipe your face or blow your nose with it. If anything bothers you that badly, excuse yourself to the restroom.

- When eating at someone's home or as a guest at a restaurant, always thank the host and tell them how delicious it was, even if it was not. Someone took time, energy, and expense to prepare the food – show your appreciation.

- It's okay to put your elbows on the table if you're not actually eating. But, if you're eating, then only rest the forearms on the table.

You can also inculcate good manners by playing a game of 'Mannerisms' over a series of nights. Ask your kids to select a manner card at the start of each meal and focus on that manner that night. And you can further tailor the game to your family. Some samples are, if your kids are motivated by reward, affix stickers to the manner card successfully accomplished. If your children like competition between them, devise different rewards like the best mannered child picks his or her choice of card on the next day. You can also play cumulatively, having your children watch out for previous night's manners and keeping score on a sheet of paper. Make it a game initially. Teaching children good manners now will ensure they enjoy socialising at meal times for the rest of their lives.

When children enter school, usually around the age of five, they become more independent. Since you will not be at their side all the time, make sure your child is equipped with the necessary skills for interacting with peers and adults. Increase your expectations. By now, your child should exhibit basic table manners, greet adults and carry on a simple conversation, receive and extend a compliment, introduce family and friends, and respect the feelings of others.

Provide a prompt. If your child forgets to place her napkin on her lap, you should quietly lean over and whisper, "What are we supposed to do before we start eating?" This gives him or her the opportunity to do the right thing. Be gentle in your reminder though. Your child will be more likely to remember the right behaviour next time if you don't belittle them for a slip up.

Prepare your child for situations. Since five-to seven-year-olds are involved in adult situations, such as family reunions, meals at restaurants, and eating at a friend's house without you, be sure he or she is equipped with an understanding of appropriate manners for each of these events.

> ### Always remember...
> Children learn by example. Behave in a way you would like your child to behave and they will follow in your footsteps.
> Teach them to say 'please', 'thank you' and 'sorry' whenever it is necessary.
> Reprimand bad behaviour so they know there's a price to pay.

MEETING THE IN-LAWS

No matter how progressive we are, we are a traditional country. So when you're meeting your in-laws, no matter how cool you are, traditional always comes to the fore. Meeting your in-laws for the first time can be a daunting experience, sure to put butterflies in your stomach – but that should be your best-kept secret. You will need to strike the perfect balance between exuding confidence, and keeping any aggression under wraps. Since first impressions are sometimes last impressions, you must present a complete picture of intellectualism, elegance and confidence.

The most important thing women should do is dress conservatively. That means no figure-fitting clothes, no cleavage and no exposure. For men, this means no torn jeans, comic T-shirts, or leather jackets. Even if you know that they are very modern, maintain a respectful way of dressing. This is not the time to wow them with your cutting edge fashion sense. Make sure your hair, ears and fingernails are clean, your ears, and under your fingernails. It's not a bad idea for women to have a little makeup on and highlight their best features.

Smile! See if there's anything you can do to assist in the kitchen;

help clear and clean the dishes and you're golden. They will always remember these little, thoughtful considerate acts. Bring them a gift. That's common courtesy. Do some research on them to know what they like. Your purchase doesn't need to be large or expensive. Maybe a bottle of wine, or something for the house that your partner says they will like. Be creative and anything homemade scores points.

Walk tall and stand upright. Wear a calm, relaxed attitude, a pleasant expression and a smile that lights up your face. This sends both an I-am-in-control message and projects positive vibes. Floor them with your grace and charm. This applies to both men and women. Don't forget to be yourself; don't try to be who you think they want you to be. Assert your personality in small doses so they don't think you're someone with no opinions. But make sure the conversation doesn't turn into an argument. Sure, some parents are looking for faults, but most just want to make sure that their child is in love with a sane, sweet person and will be in good hands.

Lastly, breathe. Try to relax, and remember that everyone present is going through a transition – each of you is gaining new family members. And that's always a good thing.

> ### Always remember...
> Avoid spraying your in-laws by talking while eating.
> Involve them in conversation but skip personal questions.
> Dress conservatively.
> Don't blow your own trumpet, but make sure you speak articulately, intelligently and interestingly.

ON YOUR FIRST DATE

I want to share a story of a friend who years ago went on a date that went so horribly wrong we still laugh over it.

She was coerced into going by her friends, who wanted to pair her off with this 'perfect' guy who was of Indian origin, but had lived most of his life in the US. He was to pick her up at 8 pm. She was ready way before time when he called to say he was running late and to meet him directly at the restaurant. She was disappointed, but tried not to let this put her off. She arrived at the restaurant before him and had to wait for him alone.

He walked in 20 minutes later, apologized for being late and her irritation eased a bit. He kept chewing gum profusely and she thought that maybe he was a bit unsure of himself. That's when the drama started. He snapped his fingers, shouting, "Waiter, waiter," which thoroughly embarrassed her because most people in the restaurant turned to look at them. He took the liberty of ordering the drinks, starters and the main course without asking her what her preference was.

When the drinks arrived, he popped his gum out of his mouth with his fingers and stuck it onto the side plate. She was naturally aghast. It was not discreet or wrapped in a paper and through the entire dinner, she had this dirty chewed-up gum, staring at her from that plate. He, of course, was unfazed and oblivious of his bad table manners. They chatted, making small talk, when he started bragging about how he shops at only the best stores in every city, name-dropping designer brands. One conversation really amused her. With remarkable confidence he told her how he had just purchased something from the best ever branded store 'Nicholsons'. Puzzled about what this new name was she searched her memory for all the designer stores she knew of but couldn't fathom who or what he meant. She was in the fashion business and knew all the brands. Then, it finally dawned upon her that he meant Harvey Nichols. She wanted to giggle, but stifled it. He then became intrusive about her ex-boyfriend by asking too many personal questions, which made her increasingly uncomfortable on this ill-fated date. The final straw was when the bill came. He fiddled around in his pocket for his wallet, and then went through it admitting he had not brought enough cash for the meal, so she had no choice but to foot the bill.

You can guess the outcome of that date. I am sure that a significant number of people have had at least one of the unpleasant experiences she had that evening. It was just her rotten luck that all the things that could go wrong at a date happened to her.

Now sometimes, albeit very rarely and for the few fortunate ones, Cupid may strike instantly. But if that does

No one wants to be around a drunken date. That will guarantee you will feature in his worst date stories.

not happen, you can still be charming and enjoyable company for your date by keeping a few pointers in mind.

For women

The time and place of your date will determine your attire and your look. Opt for an easy casual style for a lunch or teatime rendezvous. For a dinner date, you can go for a more dramatic look. But remember to dress for the body you have and not the body you want.

Wear minimal makeup that subtly highlights your best features. Avoid a 'bare it all' look that exposes too much skin. Pick something that flatters your body as well as shows your sense of style. The trick is to look stylishly simple but sexy as well. Ensure hands and feet are manicured and pedicured, and don't forget to dab a subtle perfume on your pulse points.

Try not to hog the conversation. Be a good listener and pay attention by making eye contact and looking interested. Ask questions about him. When you are in doubt, ask him a question. If you are afraid the conversation will be dull, catch up on current events and pop culture as fallback topics. Most importantly, never be critical in conversation or bad-mouth anyone. Of course, keep your cell phone on silent mode and only attend to urgent or important matters.

Be considerate of what you order. Just because you are on a date does not give you a free pass to order the most expensive thing on the menu. The same goes for alcohol. Also, don't overdo on the cocktails. No one wants to be around a drunken date. That will guarantee you will feature in his worst date stories.

For men

Your appearance plays a crucial role. Please look as if you have made an effort. Make sure you shave or have a well-trimmed beard. Splash on a masculine aftershave and a dab of cologne. Trust me, well-manicured hands will add to extra brownie points.

Arrange or offer to fetch her from her home, as it is a gracious gesture and will never go unappreciated. Make sure you are on time though.

I am a firm believer in good old chivalry, so let her precede you always, open doors and pull the occasional chair for her. I can say quite confidently that most women would be floored by such attention, especially when it is unexpected! This would also extend to not using locker room language however cool it may be, cursing and swearing isn't your prerogative as a man! Be focused on the conversation and do not let your eyes stray around the room. Be charming but not forward – respect her privacy and her space.

> **Always remember...**
>
> Dress comfortably.
> Men should be chivalrous and women considerate.
> Be on time. People judge on first dates and keeping the other person waiting won't earn you any brownie points.

MOVING ON AFTER A BREAKUP

How do you gracefully move out of someone's life when a relationship ends? This stage is a true test of one's dignity. All breakups are hard, but you are an adult, not a petulant child. So you have to teach yourself to keep your chin up and your dignity intact. Different people seem to handle this situation in different ways. But depending on your inner strength, there are two ways to cope with it. You can either make a clean break, leave the past behind and close the chapter. Or you take your time and deal with fluctuating emotions. Good breakup etiquette actually serves everyone's best interests, including yours, because you will carry less baggage into your next relationship.

Don't name-call: By the time the two of you have decided to call it quits, everything has already been said and done. Sure, a year from that point, you may have new insight about the relationship, but those will not come until you have time for peace and reflection. When you allow things to get ugly, it shows a final attempt at immediate gratification. We all know of couples who have had a nasty breakup and who call each other the filthiest of names – sometimes in the presence of their children. How is that civilized, when you abuse their mother or father in front of them?

Tell them you will miss them: No matter how upsetting a relationship may have been, both partners will have moments where they will miss each other because there was once an attachment. Telling them that a part of you will miss them acknowledges that you spent an important part of your life together and that there was love in that relationship.

Check if they are okay: Usually, it's best to not get into a back and forth, so leave it at one or two emails and then let it go. Sending an email a month or so after the breakup asking if they're doing fine is a kind way to show that you haven't forgotten about your partner.

> **Always remember...**
>
> Greet your ex's family or friends with the same warmth and feeling as you once did. They will recognize the maturity and decency of your action. Letting go sometimes is the best option.

BUMPING INTO AN EX

This scenario is likely to happen at some point. You may avoid your ex by not going to the places he or she is likely to go to. But there will come a time when you accidentally meet him or her somewhere. Hiding is out of the question because you are not a petulant or scared child. Deal with the matter like an adult. How you behave at that time will show how much you have grown. Here are a few ways to deal with the uncomfortable situation in a mature manner.

Say hello: This is something that can help you get the advantage in the awkward moment. You don't need to be rude or pretend as if both of you don't even exist. So be the first to wave hello. That way you are making sure, you make the first move. And that would make it seem as if you're not feeling awkward about the situation. And since you waved your hand already, there's no more pressure on you to do anything beyond that. All you need to do is smile, look in your ex's direction for a second or two, and wait to see what he or she does to reciprocate your hello. Does he or she just

> Even if there's a lot left you want to say to an ex, a casual run-in is not the time or place. Ask how they are doing and about their health and try to end the conversation on a good note.

wave back and look away? Or does your ex smile brightly and walk towards you?

Keep it short and sweet: If your ex does wave back, then get ready for a few minutes of small talk. Even if there's a lot left you want to say to an ex, a casual run-in is not the time or place. Ask how they are doing and about their health and try to end the conversation on a good note.

Be respectful: It's tempting to try to make your ex jealous or to publicly flirt with someone else, but you need to keep in mind that breakups are hard on everyone involved. So don't be spiteful or sarcastic, after a couple of minutes, say your goodbyes, and make a dignified exit.

WHEN SOMEONE ASKS FOR MONEY

This is probably one of the most common awkward social situations you can get into. The world is made up of all kinds of people; some who are good at managing their money and others who live on a credit policy. They borrow, in cash or kind, from neighbours, family and friends. In an ideal scenario, it is best to keep your distance from them. But since that doesn't always happen, learn to deal with the person and situation smartly.

I have seen many examples where these lending arrangements have caused considerable grief and anxiety for the lender. What starts out as a helpful deed based on love, trust and promises can lead to bad feelings, arguments, loss and severed relationships. Here are some simple principles to protect yourself and preserve your relationships:

1. Fix a return date. If and when you do lend something, confirm the duration for which it is required and the date it will be returned.

2. Inform the person that, should they default in repayment, an interest, in cash or kind, will be charged on a daily basis. A slab of chocolates for tiny 'favours' is fair.

3. When lending a significant amount of money, treat it as a proper business transaction, rather than an oral agreement or a promise. A proper written repayment plan should be drawn up, putting the terms of the loan down on paper makes clear

to all involved exactly what is expected of them. Both parties should sign the document and keep copies. This includes a friend or a family member.

4. Learn to say no. How you say it will reflect how others see you. Be upfront and direct when dealing with others. When you must say 'no', do so firmly yet gently. I know it's never easy to say no to family or friends, but if you really can't, be honest and don't make up excuses about why you can't front the cash. Instead, offer to be a reference or introduce them to someone who can help, depending on the situation. This way, you are still helping, just not as their personal banker.

5. Don't ever lend money that you can't afford to lose. If you are dependent on the borrower making repayments, then keep in mind that you are taking a big risk. There is a high default rate on loans to family and friends, so be prepared for the worst.

THE ART OF GIFTING

A gift is meant to show that you care about the person you are giving it to. A good gift shows that you get them. A present that is not given purely for the joy of giving can never be called a present in the first place.

The key is to select gifts that will make the recipient excited. I often consider the person's hobbies and interests before I select the perfect present. However, the real key to gifting is personalisation. Even if you end up with the same gift as someone else, for example, towels, you will always have the unique touch with some personalisation. A personal gift should be occasion-driven.

For a wedding: Money is considered an acceptable gift in most cultures. In fact, it is the most practical and well appreciated, and it is preferable to receiving gifts that neither matches the décor nor is one-of-a-kind. However, if you are aware of the couple's requirements or the décor of their home, gift a household item that they could remember you by. When gifting money, always present it in a decorative but sealed envelope. Abroad, the idea of wedding showers and couples who put out a gift registry ensures that they receive useful gifts. To me, this makes a lot of sense. Invitations that request no presents should be honoured.

For a business associate: Ensure you don't give something personal like underwear. Instead, you can give a monogrammed pen, something they can use at work, a photo frame or stationery. If you are attending a business party in the evening, chocolates, savouries or flowers are always a good idea. You can take a bottle of wine if you are sure you are not hurting their religious sentiments.

For children: Books are really the best gift for kids of all ages. Choose books classified for the precise age group. In my opinion, gifting apparel is dicey unless you are certain of the size.

Always give what you can afford. Just because the person you are gifting to is wealthy doesn't mean you have to stretch yourself. Gift within your means.

The one thing to remember while gifting is to be careful while recycling gifts. Ideally, we should never recycle. But everybody does it. And that's fine. You would rather someone use the gift than it just lying around in your house. If you are going to recycle, make sure it's in good condition. Otherwise, the receiver will know it's recycled and that just leaves a bad taste in their mouth. Another mistake people make is thinking their gift is not good enough. There is as much pleasure in giving as there is in receiving; never be ashamed of what you gift. So they add more gifts so it looks bigger. It says that you don't think your gift is good and you're trying too hard to make up for it. Also, don't give inappropriate gifts. Just because something is lying around in your house, it does not mean it should do the same in someone else's house.

Packaging a gift the right way is equally important. You can make a modest gift look much grander if you pack it well. A beautifully wrapped gift is always a pleasure to receive. There are countless ways to choose a good gift, but the best gift is one that is personal.

I would like to end this by citing an example of how not to behave when it comes to gifts. We attended a destination wedding recently and the bride and groom had kept thank you gifts for all their guests in our individual rooms. That was such a lovely gesture and they were kind enough to let us know that if we did not like the colour of the gift, we could exchange it if there were leftovers. One of their guests took advantage of the opportunity and stuffed all the surplus gifts in her bag. She took all the extra gifts for herself! The woman in question still does not know that the hosts know what she did. It is the graciousness of the hosts that she has not been put in an awkward situation. Don't ever put greed before etiquette because sooner or later you will be found out.

> **Always remember...**
>
> Get a gift that is appropriate for that function you are attending. Be careful while recycling a gift. You don't want it to be an embarrassment for you or the receiver.

CONDOLENCES

Now, this is a touchy topic. But expressing condolences the right way is extremely important because we all experience death. One of the reasons why people are so uncomfortable after someone passes away is because they are not sure about what to do or say. While death may be an extremely uncomfortable topic, the worst thing you can do is ignore it when it occurs in the family of someone you know. Doing nothing, or pretending it didn't happen, is just not done.

How you offer condolences depends on how close you are to the person. If it's an immediate family member, you have to be with them throughout. But if it's an acquaintance, you don't need to be with them all the time. If you are unable to meet them in person, give them a call. Keep the conversation brief because the family is likely to be deluged with phone calls. Also, keep the focus on the bereaved and the person who has passed away. This is not the time to relate your own experience with losing a loved one.

My uncle passed away recently and the entire day my aunt had visitors who came and met her. By evening, she was so tired of entertaining that she snapped and she requested them to leave. That's why it is a good idea to call someone in the know and ask when it is a good time to visit. This is also why there are prayer meetings. They give the grieving family a break from the constant flow of visitors and there is a set time for concerned people to meet them. After my uncle passed away, I sent messages to everyone who knew

> Be a good listener. The bereaved may want to vent, cry, or grieve. Let them talk. Similarly, if they don't want to talk about it, don't pressure them.

him so that first they would know that he had passed away and they would know the time and date of the prayer meeting.

The simplest way is to say, "I'm so sorry for your loss." It's not kind to ask what happened, whether he suffered, or say, "It was his time to go." It's extremely rude to dwell on the illness or manner of death. I have seen so many people do this. Just speak from your heart in your own words. Don't ask questions about the circumstances or probe for details about the death. Instead, tell them that you are just a phone call away if they need you. Offer your services. Maybe they want a meal cooked, or their child picked up from school. That will take a load off their shoulders. A grieving family should not be busy cooking for guests or serving them tea or coffee. Maybe you could chip in at that time and do that for them. Be a good listener. The bereaved may want to vent, cry, or grieve. Let them talk. Similarly, if they don't want to talk about it, don't pressure them.

Always remember to dress appropriately for the funeral. If you have come to know about the death when you are at work and you are not dressed conservatively, buy a stole to cover your shoulders. Different communities have different rituals. Hindu and Parsi mourners wear white at funerals; Muslims and Christians wear black. Follow these customs. Make sure your mobile phone is switched off at the funeral. I cannot even begin to say how rude that is. Step out and take the call if you really need to take it. People also tend to talk at prayer meetings. Yes, they can be long and tedious. But I am sure you can curb yourself for an hour. Show some respect.

If you have been asked to make a speech at the service, make it short and meaningful. The idea is to focus on the person who has passed away. At a prayer meet I went to, one gentleman spoke for so long – even about his childhood experiences with the deceased. The focus of the speech became his own grieving and not the departed.

You may feel that the family needs their space and time to grieve; send a sympathy letter or card as soon as you hear about the bereavement. Most of us resort to the mechanical responses on printed cards. To me, this is extremely impersonal. A sympathy card or letter should be a personal expression, handwritten in blue or black ink, on your personal stationery or on white or ivory paper. Writing a sympathy letter is quite difficult, but the longer you put it off, the more difficult it becomes. These tips will help make the writing easier: keep it short, simple, sincere and honest. The purpose of the letter is to give solace to the bereaved. It's never too late to offer sympathy, love and support to a friend during a time of great sadness, even if you hear about the death weeks later. It will always be comforting to the recipient if you share a personal memory of the person who died in the letter. If the deceased person had lived in another town, an immediate short email, expressing your sympathy, would be appropriate. But it must be followed by a personal handwritten letter. On no account should you send a sympathy text message. Even a simple phone call after the funeral lets the family know you care. Remember that the months following a death are when grieving friends and family need support the most.

The don'ts of funeral etiquette

Don't bring your cell phone: Your phone ringing is highly inappropriate and will cause a disturbance, so turn any ringers or notifications off. It will be even better to leave your phone at home because a funeral is not the time to be texting or checking your messages.

Don't be afraid to remember the good times: Funerals are obviously a time of grieving and mourning, but remembering the good times helps with the healing process. Sharing a funny and appropriate story is acceptable, and in some cases, exactly what the deceased would have wanted and will give the grieving family some relief.

It is common not to know what to say or how to act, and as a result, many people shy away from engaging with people who are grieving. Especially at a funeral or condolence meeting, where there may be many people in attendance, it can be easy to feel like you don't want to crowd or overwhelm the bereaved. It's important to remember, though, that people who are grieving still need your love, attention, and support, and that these are all things you can offer.

> **Always remember...**
> Just an 'I'm sorry for your loss' is enough. The person grieving wants a friend by their side. Be that.
> Don't ask how they passed away or say that it's for the best. That is very insensitive.

EMAIL ETIQUETTE

Research by McKinsey Global Institute and International Data Corp has found that we spend about a quarter of our time at work combing through and answering the emails we send and receive each day. Email is the second-most time-consuming activity for workers, next to 'role-specific tasks'. For an activity that important, we still don't know how to use it appropriately. But there's a fair amount of protocol that goes with it too. How personal is too personal? What about your e-signature? How much information should it contain? What is the line between personal and professional emails; how much monitoring do both need in terms of content, length, emoticons, abbreviations or exclamations? Is there something like being 'too proper' too? That's why there have to be some rules that we all follow to ensure there's no miscommunication.

Use a professional email address: Begin by using your company email address if you work for one. But many people use their personal email address at work because of its large storage space. That's fine, but be careful while choosing that address. We all had some cheesy ones when email was new – someone I know had her favourite Hollywood actor's name even though she was a woman. But you're a working professional and email address like 'party girl' and 'football maniac' are not appropriate. Just go with your name – first name and then last name.

Address people professionally: Don't use laid-back, colloquial expressions like, 'Hey Pooja', or 'Yo Rahul'. 'Hey' is a very informal word and it should not be used in the workplace. Use Hi or Hello instead. Similarly, don't end the email with 'Love, Megha'. The closing phrase at the end of the email should be 'Best Regards', 'Sincerely', or 'Thank You'. This also applies when you receive a casual email. Just because the sender is informal does not mean you have to be too. Reply in a professional manner. Take a deep breath before you send a nasty reply to a nasty email. A rude reply can make the things worse.

Type the correct name: You would think I wouldn't have to mention this. But it is a fairly common mistake people make. I know a girl called Upneet, but most of the emails she gets are addressed to 'Puneet'. This happens even when they are replying to a email Upneet has sent and which, hence, has her correct name mentioned. While she is used to people making such mistakes, it's still not okay to make them. People tend to remember when you mispronounce or mistype their name and you don't want that held against you, especially in a professional capacity.

Write a direct subject line: People often decide whether to open an email based on the subject line. Choose one that lets the recipient know you are addressing their concerns or that it's an email that needs to be read urgently.

BCC the recipients: When sending an email, some people place all the email addresses in the To: field. If the recipient list is large, that means that all your readers will have to scroll through the list of on the 'To' field to read the message. This can be very irritating, especially if they are checking the email on their smartphone. You also have to consider that others may not want their email address published for everyone to see. Avoid both these issues by using the BCC option.

Don't try to be funny: Humour can easily get lost in translation because the recipient may not understand your tone or your facial expressions. It's better to leave humour out of emails unless you know the recipient well. Also, something that you think is funny might not be funny to someone else. Don't use smiley faces either.

Don't 'Reply all': No one wants to read emails from twenty people when it has nothing to do with them. They could just ignore the emails, but many people get notifications of new messages on their smartphones or distracting pop-up messages on their computer screens. Refrain from hitting 'reply all' unless you really think everyone on the list needs to receive the email, says Barbara Pachter in her book, *The Essentials of Business Etiquette*. I agree completely.

But reply to all emails: It's difficult to reply to every email message ever sent to you, but you should try to. Remember all those times you sent out emails and didn't get any replies? Remember how dejected you felt and mentally chided them for not having basic manners? Well, learn from that, and reply to the emails you receive. This includes even those emails accidentally sent to you, especially if the sender is expecting a reply. A reply isn't necessary, but serves as good email etiquette, especially if this person works in the same company or industry as you. Even a simple, "I don't think you meant to send this email to me. And I wanted to let you know so you can send it to the correct person," is enough.

Check the grammar: This is unpardonable. Grammatical mistakes and spelling errors never go unnoticed and you will be judged. I always read and reread my email at least twice before pressing the send button. Someone told me about how she intended to write 'Sorry for the inconvenience'. But she didn't pay attention to the spell-check and ended up sending 'Sorry for the incontinence'. It's funny now, but I would be mortified if I was in her place. Also, don't write an email in all capital letters. That conveys that you are angry and are shouting your message. An accountant at a company in the UK was sacked after colleagues complained that her emails were too 'shouty' and confrontational because she would always type in capitals. Now you don't want to be in that situation, do you?

Add the email address last: I have learnt this from experience. You don't want to send an email accidentally before you have finished writing and proofing the message. Sometimes this results in the embarrassing situation of sending an unfinished email. Even when you are replying to a message, delete the recipient's address and add it only when you are sure you are ready to send the reply.

WHEN YOU ARE A NEWLYWED

I know of a family whose daughter had been raised with the best of things around her. They found a suitable boy for her in England when she was quite young – that's how it's done in their community – and they got married. Within one month, she said she was done with the marriage and came back home to India. She said that she found it difficult to adjust there because they did things differently in her husband's house. Instead of working it out and giving herself time to adjust, the family encouraged her to move back home.

I feel very sad every time I think of this because she gave up on a marriage so easily. She didn't even give it a shot. She, and her family, failed to realize that a marriage is always going to be difficult for you initially, but you don't give up on something as important as marriage so soon. That's the most important thing I can tell a new bride.

You are going to a new house. And no home in the world will be like your parents. So open your mind to new possibilities. Once you have moved in, one way to break the ice is by offering help. Ask if you can help with the kitchen. Maybe watering the plants every day can be your responsibility now. This shows that you are making an effort to gel with them. But don't be too pushy. People run their homes in a particular way. Try to blend in, instead of suggesting drastic changes. Go about it subtly. If you want to make changes, go about it gradually. Say, there's a vase in the living room that you think is hideous. It's a bad idea to just say so and tell them that it should be removed. Instead, why not buy another vase and suggest alternating between the two vases. Maybe they will realize theirs was quite unsightly and yours looks much better with the interiors of the home.

Of course, you have to be nice to everyone. But that doesn't mean you have to be a pushover. Never be afraid to voice your opinion, especially if you notice that someone is being unfair. They may not realize it then, but everyone appreciates an honest person.

> Never be afraid to voice your opinion, especially if you notice that someone is being unfair. They may not realize it then, but everyone appreciates an honest person.

Since you and the family are all new to this whole gamut of relationships, there's bound to be friction. But don't complain to your husband every time you have a problem with something. Try solving things out yourself. Also, as humans, we tend to focus on what is missing or lacking in a relationship and overlook or fail to appreciate what it might be giving us. Try not to do that.

New grooms, too, should keep a few things in mind. Your wife has left her house and all things that are dear to her and has come to yours. So it's your job to make the journey smooth for her. I am a Parsi and my husband is a Muslim. I am very religious and my husband is not. But he's never stopped me from doing what I wanted to do or following whatever faith I choose to follow. That kind of sensitivity is very important.

Another common mistake husbands make is compare their wives to their mothers. And more often than not, the wives always lose. Don't do that. Your wife is her own person and deserves to be treated as one.

Always remember...

Be courteous and tactful when dealing with tricky situations.
Don't compare your spouse to your parent. Both have specific roles in your life and don't confuse those.

DEALING WITH ILL-MANNERED PEOPLE

This is the one thing where I advocate getting rude. When someone is verbally abusing you or physically assaulting you, you have the right to tell them to shut up. I went to a restaurant recently with some people. One of the men in our group was in a foul mood and kept treating the waiters badly. Behaving badly with someone who cannot do the same in return shows the kind of person you are. I had to tell him to mind his manners. Yes, we all get angry. But you have to learn to deal with it. Abusing someone else is just not done. I see so many people on the streets so angry while driving. Yes, I understand road rage, but there is really no need to hurl abuses at each other like the way some people do.

When two people are fighting, the best thing to do is to separate them. Be an intervener and take them to different rooms. That will

When two people are fighting, the best thing to do is to separate them. Be an intervener and take them to different rooms. That will give both of them a time out and cool them down.

give both of them a time out and cool them down.

Be respectful of gender, race, religion, political viewpoints and other potentially controversial or difficult subjects. Do not make derogatory or potentially inflammatory comments. It's such conversations that lead to fights and abuse.

GYM ETIQUETTE

The gym is increasingly becoming a place most of us visit every day. It's important to remember that there is a certain sense of decorum to follow when you're in a communal workout space. While every gym has its own set of rules, everyone should follow some general etiquette guidelines.

If you are sick, stay home: Coughing and sneezing during a fitness class or while lifting weights leaves a trail of germs waiting to infect the rest of the gym. If you have a sore throat or a cold, that's usually okay. Working out in that condition will not affect your health. But be mindful that not everyone will feel that way – your fellow gym-goers may frown upon that. It's best to opt for a home workout. However, if you do want to go to the gym, make sure you sanitize all equipment you use properly. Actually, you should do this even if you are feeling well.

Focus on you: Every gym has people who flirt, or try to at least. Then there are people who stare and hover around the neighbour's treadmill. Don't do that. When you are at the gym, your time should be spent focusing on your own workout, not anyone else's. You should be paying attention to what *you* are doing

Dress appropriately: Short shorts, barely-there tank tops and loose, baggy clothes that can get caught in a machine can all constitute gym hazards. I have seen both men and women pop out of their too-tight clothes. That's not a sight anyone wants to see. Moreover, it does not aid your workout and you just end up being uncomfortable. Similarly, baggy clothing or pants that are too long can get caught on something or you can trip over them and injure yourself.

Use deodorant: Leave fragrances and colognes for outside the gym, but inside, use a deodorant. Heavy fragrances and perfumes can be distracting to your fellow gym goers. Strong body odour can also be very unpleasant. My former personal trainer had once told me that several women use lotions before a workout. That's a bad idea because creams make your skin slippery, making it difficult to hold your posture or to your equipment. You also need to bring a towel to the gym, wipe your benches down after you are done with them.

Keep unsolicited advice to yourself: No one likes being told what to do, especially from a know-it-all stranger. So keep your opinions to yourself. If you are not a certified fitness professional, offering fitness advice is not in your job description. If you see someone performing an exercise that is likely to injure them, talk to a trainer and let them know what you observed. The trainer will know how to approach people in a proper manner.

Respect other people's space: The gym is a place where people enjoy spending time with themselves. So don't start conversations unless the other person seems genuinely interested. Also, stay off your phone. No one wants to hear your conversations. If there is an urgent call that needs your attention, exit the training area. You will probably have better reception and more privacy outside, and the people around you will appreciate it.

Don't hog equipment: Every time I go to the gym, I encounter at least one machine that has a towel hanging off it. When I was a gym novice, I used to think that someone had forgotten their towel. Now I know that the towel means that the equipment is booked. Leaving your towel hanging on a machine does not give you dibs on that piece of equipment. This is an absolute no-no when others are waiting to work out. You should also step off after your designated time is up. It's not fair to the person waiting to exercise after you. And don't forget to put the equipment back in place once you're done. If you are strong enough to lift the weight in the first place, you are strong enough to set it back down where you found it. Always re-rack the weights for the next person, and keep the gym organized.

ELEVATORS AND SUPERMARKET ETIQUETTE

The first sight everyone sees as soon as they enter their workplace is a crowd of people waiting for the elevator. And when it rings, announcing its arrival, everyone runs to rush in. The urge to not waste even a couple of minutes for the next one to arrive results in some impolite, rude behaviour. Why anyone would want to start his or her workday on such a sour note is something I will never understand. Here's how you can get it right and at least your long, stressful day a good beginning.

It is always nice to acknowledge the elevator attendant whose mundane but responsible job it is to make sure that all the passengers are transported safe to their respective floors. He is probably the only person who is in a position to rescue you if the elevator is stuck between floors. So do remember to spare a moment for him. Don't forget that you aren't the only one in that space. Be considerate and call for the elevator only when you are ready to use it. It is not fair to keep it waiting, especially if there are other passengers in it. Allow people to exit the elevator before entering.

Once you have boarded the elevator, indicate your floor, do not always take it for granted that the attendant will know where you want to go. If you need to talk to other people inside, speak softly. That is applicable for when you are on your cell phone too. Loud sounds can be very jarring in small spaces. Cover your mouth and excuse yourself if you sneeze, cough, yawn or burp in this small space, and do not even think of passing wind in the elevator.

When you have touched ground, exit quickly and do not linger near the doorway. And, of course, a small thank you to the attendant would be nice. I will end this with a story someone shared with me. "I work at a major MNC where some of the finest minds of the country are hired. I take the elevator at least twice a day. That's about forty times a month. Of those forty encounters with other people, perhaps one man a month will let me step in the elevator first or off the elevator first. The other thirty-nine rush in and out with no concern for me or other women on the elevator. People work so hard to select the proper car, the proper suit, the latest cell phone, yet they give no thought to the fact that their manners, for lack of a more appropriate word,

> Speak quickly and do not hold up the store attendants or other shoppers while on the phone and, of course, speak softly.

suck."

Now for a little retail therapy.

How many romance movies have we watched where a boy and girl meet in a store, bicker over grabbing the last packet of yoghurt, and then fall in love? In real life, that's a scene itching for a fight. Behaving well in a supermarket is important; especially because that's a place you are likely to visit on a regular basis. You want them to have a good opinion of you, don't you? That is why you should be polite to the store attendant and browse around until you really need assistance. If children accompany you, instruct them to stay close to you, not touch the displayed products and keep an eye on them throughout. Tell them to mind themselves if they are being a nuisance to fellow shoppers.

Do not monopolize shopping space and products. We have all, in haste, knocked over a couple of items from the shelf. Make sure you keep the items back. At the payment counter, stand in the queue and don't ask the person after you to hold the cart while you go back to grab some more items.

Speak quickly and do not hold up the store attendants or other shoppers while on the phone and, of course, speak softly. Keep an eye on the billing register to ensure that the entries are accurate. If you do notice a discrepancy, politely ask for the same to be corrected.

If at any time, you discover that an item is out of your budget, do not hesitate to return it to its shelf. What you choose to buy is entirely your prerogative, so don't feel embarrassed to do so. Before you leave, thank the attendants if they are nearby.

Always remember...

Don't try to push your way into an elevator. Let the occupants alight first and then get on.

Cover your mouth and excuse yourself if you sneeze, cough, yawn or burp in this small space.

The supermarket is for everyone to use, so don't hog the spaces.

Wait for your turn at the payment counter.

BATHROOM ETIQUETTE

Clean amenities are a fundamental right of every citizen of the world. It should be mandatory for toilet training to be included in school curriculums. There appears to be a dichotomy of sorts here though. It is truly incomprehensible how our homes are well kept, but public property doesn't warrant the same consideration. Today, the humble toilet has given way to the washroom, which functions as a 'restroom' (a place where a person can rest their feet and freshen up). It's increasingly important, therefore, that the area is clean and pleasant.

While most of the loos in our homes are clean, it's when we use public restrooms, especially at work, that the problems arise. Remember that you are not the only person using the restroom at the workplace. There are other employees as well. It is essential to keep public toilets clean and hygienic to avoid transmission of germs and infections.

Never leave the restroom dirty. A sign in one of the offices I visited recently said, 'Flush and flush until all is clear, so the next may have no fear.' Leave the restroom as clean as you would want it to be when you enter. Lock the door carefully when you are inside.

If someone is inside, don't peep under the doors or knock endlessly. Wait for the other person to come out. Make sure you do not wet the toilet seat. Do not throw water on the floor as someone might slip and get hurt. Women should always sit on the toilet seat while peeing and men should always stand a little close to the toilet seat to avoid dripping. Never forget to flush once you are done. Check the toilet seat for unwanted stains or substance. Call the toilet attendant if the flush is not working. Make sure you do not throw anything in the commode. Tissue paper must be thrown inside the dustbin and not anywhere else. Sanitary napkins must be wrapped in polythene bags and disposed in dustbins. Don't take more time than required because there are people waiting for their turn.

Wash your hand with an antiseptic soap or sanitizer every time you use the restroom. Use tissue paper to wipe off hands. Wash basins must be used for washing hands and face only. I once walked in on a woman washing her feet in the basin. When I told her to stop doing that, she blamed the monsoon season. It was quite a sight to walk into. Make sure the water does not splash outside the sink.

Should that happen, wipe it. Do not leave the restroom with taps on. Conserve water. Don't comb your hair over the sink and leave strands behind and don't blow your nose in the washbasin. Use a tissue and throw it in the bin. Don't spit on the floor. If you spit paan juice in the sink, wash the stain away with plenty of water.

SOCIAL MEDIA ETIQUETTE

Social media etiquette is the most requested theme I have gotten in the recent past because it's such a huge part of our lives now. Very few people are not on any social media sites. Since it's such a new topic, it took me some time to fully understand the ins and outs. Then I realized that it is no different than talking to people in different real-life situations. The same polite behaviour applies on social media as well.

Don't be a know-it-all: It's nice to have something valuable to say, but what people dislike online is self-acclaimed experts in every field. I'm sure you don't know everything about Indian politics, David Bowie or Uzbekistan's foreign affairs. So don't pretend you do.

Don't get into arguments: I can't emphasize this enough, especially in the current political scenario where people have already taken sides and anyone on the other side is an enemy. Social media is a great source, not only for news, but also for exchanging views. Even if you don't agree with others, don't let it turn into a nasty argument. And if you do get into an argument, say whatever it is you have to say and leave. Don't call anyone names.

Censor yourself: Some people treat their Facebook or Twitter accounts as diaries. But please don't share everything with your followers. Some things are meant to be kept private and let's keep it that way. A Facebook acquaintance constantly posts about how her relationships aren't working and sad poems and thoughts about how heartbroken she is. Matters of the heart are not something that should be discussed over Facebook. No one comments on her posts online, but offline, they have a lot to say. Why put yourself in that position where people gossip about you?

Don't post party photos all the time: Yes, you want to tell everyone about the fun you had last night. However, bear in mind that potential employers now check people's social media accounts to get an idea of the kind of person they are. A 2012 technology market survey conducted by Eurocom Worldwide and the Global PR Network found that 40 per cent of the tech companies surveyed said they look at potential employees' profiles on social media sites. "The fact that one in five applicants are disqualified from an interview because of content in the social media sphere is a warning to job seekers and a true indicator of the digital reality we now live in," the survey said. In fact, a high school teacher from the American state of Georgia, was forced to resign after posting pictures of herself drinking on the social networking site. She was told her page 'promoted alcohol use' and 'contained profanity'. So learn from her experience and be careful about what you post.

MAINTAINING PERSONAL SPACE

I have a friend who has this awful habit of looking in the phone of the person next to her as they type. And she will always have some funny comment to make on what she's read. While this is fine occasionally, people didn't like it as she always did that. Maintaining someone's privacy and personal space is the least you can do for someone. People have shared experiences of colleagues standing over them, who read while they typed or worked, and sometimes even read their emails. A friend was in a ferry once, checking photographs on her digital camera, when some random guy started peeping into the pictures. He even commented on one of them, saying they looked like a happy family. I am sure there are those who open others' letters and mail and relatives or friends who pick up cell phone calls and read messages.

Many people, especially those living in big cities, don't realize when they're standing too close to someone. A three-foot radius is what constitutes that personal space, the invasion of which is irritatingly

Mail of any sort is personal and private and it is extremely bad manners to read another's email unless specifically asked to do so. In fact, even spouses should respect each other's privacy and leave the other's email alone.

rude and rather uncouth.

Observing boundaries in the office is important to maintaining professionalism. After working with people for years and getting to know them, these lines may have become blurred. But others who don't know you well, including supervisors, may misunderstand your behaviour. That is why you should observe professional distance while at the office. When a colleague reads your email or letter over your shoulder or peers at your phone messages, a simple but subtle, "Can I help you?" or "Do you want something?" will indicate that you are offended by their intrusive behaviour. Exposed and off balance, they will sheepishly retreat. At the same time, you will allow them to save face. If the person still doesn't take the hint, you need to be blunt. Minimize the window you are working on or place your papers under cover and pointedly turn your attention to the person.

Dr Lois Frankel, author and an executive coach who travels the world coaching CEOs and senior management of some of the biggest companies, says, "While offices aren't exactly homes, they should be treated with the same kind of respect." We are unlikely to enter someone's home uninvited, pick up and read their mail, aren't we? The same courtesy therefore should be extended in the workplace. I suggest posting a humorous sign that designates desk items as off limits. Mail of any sort is personal and private and it is extremely bad manners to read another's mail unless specifically asked to do so. In fact, even spouses should respect each other's privacy and leave the other's mail alone.

HOW TO HANDLE THE SITUATION

When someone gets uncomfortably close to you, there are several things you can do. Being direct, however, can hurt the other person's feelings, so before speaking your mind, determine whether the issue is worth bringing up.

1. Lean away from the person or take a step back, hoping they will take the hint.

2. Come right out and say you are uncomfortable being so close.

3. Explain why you need more space. For example, if you are left-handed, and the person is too close to your left side, comment about how you need the space to take notes.

PERSONAL
GROOMING

Taking care of yourself – your clothes, hygiene and nutrition – is of utmost importance. Few things can top the need for good hygiene in your life. Good personal grooming and keeping yourself neat and clean shows that you have respect for yourself and the people you meet throughout the day. There are many aspects of grooming and personal hygiene, including hair, nails, breath, body odour and clothing. Regardless of whether you are running errands or going on a job interview, good grooming should be second nature. Practising a daily routine of personal hygiene helps you put your best foot forward, no matter what the situation is.

Sometimes despite being hygienic, the toxins in our body emit bad body odour. This could be due to our diet, an illness, not drinking enough water, stress, hormones, etc. Sadly, most people who have body odour are unaware of it, as they are used to living with it. The key here is to control it with awareness. According to research conducted by the University of California, Berkeley, US, we form an opinion of someone after meeting them for the first time within the first 30 seconds. While some of that opinion is based on what they say, the majority (55 per cent) is shaped by their appearance. No doubt, wardrobe plays an important role in appearance, but it's often personal grooming and hygiene that make the biggest impression.

Everyone knows from the time we went to school that cleanliness is next to godliness. But what exactly does that involve? In matters regarding grooming, it would entail being neat, clean and presentable. Your hair should be washed and styled, and clothes, shoes and accessories should be well matched and in good condition. I will talk about the importance of looking good in detail a little later in this section. But personal hygiene is a topic that needs to be addressed immediately and is unfortunately much neglected. This is applicable to both men and women in equal measure. This requires that we take a bath at least once a day, wash our hair, brush our teeth properly and remove excessive visible facial and body hair. All this seems like a no-brainer, but you will be surprised at the number of people who don't keep themselves clean every day.

Use deodorant: Many people don't realize the difference between a deodorant and an antiperspirant. A deodorant gets rid of odour caused by sweating, while antiperspirants actually stop and dry up perspiration. Make sure you apply them on clean dry armpits after taking a bath. Go with whatever works best for you and make sure the fragrance isn't too overpowering. A common mistake people make is applying deodorant on wet armpits. That will not help your cause. Take some tissue, pat your armpits dry and only then re-apply a deodorant. Another alternative is to apply talcum powder. It's great for absorbing sweat.

Wash your face twice a day:
This is not only an important personal hygiene rule, but also a critical aspect of health. But never use soap, body gels, or body scrubs on your face. While it may be the cheapest way to go and convenient when you are in the shower, using soap and water will strip your skin of essential moisture and upset its natural pH balance, leaving it irritated and dry. Using a face cleanser that will normalize your pH and restore the moisture balance.

Hit the shower:
Shower every day first thing in the morning and at night, particularly if you have had a long day where you have worked for more than 12 hours. Bathe every time you exercise or perspire.

Clip your nails:
When it comes to men's hygiene, one of the things that attract a woman are clean, groomed nails. If your nails are long enough to collect dirt, they are too long. Trim your cuticles. And use hand lotion or cream to keep them soft and prevent calluses and cracking. Women tend to have longer nails, but that doesn't mean they can't be clean. Keep them filed and have regular manicures.

Get rid of excessive hair:
Women with excessive, visible facial and body hair need to have it removed. There are several options available these days so there is no excuse to be out and about with your body hair showing. Men should be clean-shaven or have their moustache and beards neatly trimmed.

Say no to BO and bad breath:
While talking about general hygiene, I remember an incident. My daughter has a friend who is not very hygienic. She visits our home often and when the two of them are watching TV in the room, I sometimes serve them lunch there. After she has done eating, my daughter will get off the bed to

wash her hands, but her friend just licks her fingers dry and then she is done. It is so disgusting because she will touch everything with those unwashed hands. You have to be mindful of such things, especially when you are in someone else's home. Washing your hands with soap before and after eating, as well as after visiting the bathroom is non-negotiable.

I was on an international night flight and I had to attend an important meeting when it landed the following morning. My fellow passenger happened to be a school friend who was in a chatty mood. I was excited about talking to her after so many years. But she had the worst mouth odour. And what was worse was that she was totally unaware of it. After an hour of sheer torture, I couldn't take it anymore and told her I needed to pop a double dose of a sleeping tablet. I never take a pill to induce sleep but her bad breath had traumatized me. The next day, I had to be shaken by an alarmed crew member to wake up just before we landed. I was disoriented and dishevelled and don't have much recollection of how the meeting went. All I knew was that I had been spared eight hours of the foulest smelling breath and I was grateful for that.

So what can we do to control bad breath and maintain good teeth and oral hygiene?

- Brush twice a day in a circular motion, which ensures that your gums are massaged properly.
- Use an even bristle toothbrush.
- Floss your teeth.
- Gargle after every meal with a mouthwash or regular water.
- Avoid foods and drinks that emit a bad odour like garlic and onions, or stain your teeth like tea, coffee and red wine.
- Although chewing gum after meals is actually good for your teeth, it is poor etiquette to do so while talking to someone. A good alternative is to pop mints in your mouth periodically.
- Drink lots of water.
- Visit a dentist once every six months.

With this arises the question of how to tell someone they are suffering from bad breath. If someone you are close to has that problem, it's your duty to tell them. You wouldn't be a good friend or family member if you let them walk around with bad breath.

1

SKINCARE AND MAKEUP

"Beauty, to me, is about being comfortable in your own skin. That or a kick-ass red lipstick."

— Gwyneth Paltrow, actor

f you notice carefully, a person with good personal grooming always seems to have a clear, even complexion. But not everyone is so lucky. For those not blessed with great skin, there's makeup to the rescue. If you do not have good skin, establish a skincare regimen that works for you. The basics like cleansing-toning-moisturising, wearing sunscreen, exercising regularly, getting good, satisfactory sleep and drinking lots of water apply to everyone. Naturally, there are periods of our lives where we don't have perfect complexions. Some of us are fighting acne. A good concealer helps mask those imperfections. Of course, do not rely just on concealer for a smooth complexion. See a dermatologist if you run out of solutions.

The idea of wearing makeup is to enhance your natural beauty. Many Indian women don't apply makeup on a daily basis. They believe makeup is only for special occasions such as weddings and parties. But there's no harm in using it every day if you use good products and have a good removal regimen. Begin by applying it on clean, washed skin. Then apply a primer. A primer is applied under your makeup to give you a flawless finish. Match the foundation to your skin tone for a natural look. Many women make the mistake of choosing a foundation that's lighter than their skin tone so they look fairer. That is a huge, huge mistake. Blend into the neck area so it does not look like your neck and face have two different colours. The key to good makeup is blending. Many celebrities in India have also made this very common mistake. The least you can use daily is kajal and lip gloss. You can go a bit more if you are working in the corporate sector. Apply blush on the apples of your cheeks and then blend it in. Wear lipstick to compliment the colour of your outfit. While extremely dark or bright colours are fine for after work, they are a complete no-no at the office.

Learn how to apply makeup properly. It may take practice. Ask a friend who knows to help you or go to a cosmetic counter in a store for advice. Do not share your brushes and sponges with anyone. That's how germs spread. Throw away your makeup after a year so your skin is always healthy.

MAKEUP EVERY WOMAN SHOULD HAVE

Just as there are fashion staples that every woman should own and wear, there are some essential makeup items she should have and use too. Sure, having an extensive cosmetic collection is fantastic, but what every woman needs are the perfect beauty basics.

Foundation: Probably the most important makeup essential is foundation because it evens out your skin tone and gives you a flawless complexion.

Concealer: It's better to have a stick concealer than a liquid one because it covers dark circles and blemishes very well. Don't forget to blend well with your fingers or a flat brush.

Blush: Blush can really brighten your appearance and give you a healthy, flushed glow. A hint of colour on your cheekbones is the perfect finishing touch to your makeup routine. Don't overdo it though. It's a common mistake that women make. It's better to have less blush on than an overdose of it.

Eyeliner: Having an eyeliner is important for those days when you want to shift your makeup from daytime to evening. Get one in black and in a retractable pencil form.

Kajal: A good, black kajal pencil gives your eyes an instant boost of energy. Your ideal pencil is one that is smudge-proof and does not run.

Eye shadow: While an eye shadow palette is essential, you don't need more than one for everyday use. I would recommend getting a basic everyday palette that is neutral in colour so that it will go with most of your clothes. If you are still confused about what to choose, remember that you can never go wrong with earth shades.

Lipstick: Day or night, red lipstick is always appropriate. With the right shade in your makeup bag, you will always have it as a fallback you can pull together in a few minutes.

Lip gloss: This gives you a casual look as against a matte lipstick that grabs everyone's attention.

While all these are items you should own, you don't need to carry them with you everywhere you go. For your handbag, all you need is good compact powder because you have already applied makeup in the morning before you have left for work, a lipstick and kajal. That will be enough to carry you through the entire day. Of course, bear in mind that these should suit your skin tone. Learn how to apply makeup because the best products in the world won't save you if you don't know how to go about applying it.

A FEW HELPFUL MAKEUP HINTS

- Take utmost care to blend colour on your face correctly. If not, it will end up looking chalky.
- If you have dry to normal skin, use liquid base makeup. Powder compacts are better for oily skin.
- With liquid base, apply small dots over your face and spread it evenly. With powders, apply using a sponge, or the balls of your fingers, always in the direction of your facial hair growth. Blend and smoothen evenly.
- Indian women are known for their mysterious eyes. Make sure you make the most of them. Emphasize them with eyeliner, kajal, mascara.
- When applying eye shadow, remember to apply light colours at the inner corner of the eye (near the nose) and darker colours towards the outer corner of the eye (near the temples).
- Eyeliner should be applied with a steady hand, thickening towards the outer corner of the eye accentuating your eye shape.
- You can use a kajal pencil in the rim of your eyes to give your

eyes more depth.

- Mascara should never be clumpy on your eyelashes. Lashes should look long and thick. To separate lashes, use an eyelash curler.

- Blusher should be used sparingly for just a hint of colour on your cheeks.

- Use a lip liner or pencil to accentuate your lips. If you have full lips, line your lips inside your actual lip line, and outside your actual lip line for thinner lips.

EATING RIGHT

Eating a healthy diet is so important for good skin. Your skin is like a grape. When it is plumped up with moisture, it looks like a grape. When you take the moisture away, the same fruit is a raisin. So you either apply moisture externally or give it the nutrients it needs from inside. The best way to do that is to have food that helps you get better skin. Here are some foods that do just that:

Pomegranates: They are packed with polyphenol antioxidants, which fight free radicals and regulate the skin's blood flow, giving it rosiness. One pomegranate or a couple of glasses of juice daily should do the trick.

Walnuts: Walnuts contain omega-3 essential fatty acids, which improve the skin's elasticity. They are also loaded with copper, which boosts collagen production. A handful of walnuts each day will improve your complexion's texture.

Green tea: It is very high in antioxidants, especially EGCG, which has proved to reduce redness. Studies have also shown that green tea helps fight inflammation. Sip at least one cup of green tea a day and fight redness.

Carrots: They are not just good for your eyesight. Carrots are great for clearing up breakouts too. The vitamin A in them helps prevent the overproduction of cells in the skin's outer layer where dead cells and sebum combine and clog pores.

Sweet potatoes: They are loaded with vitamin C, which smoothens out wrinkles. Vitamin C is essential for collagen production and the more collagen you have, the less wrinkled your skin looks. In fact, a study in *The American Journal of Clinical Nutrition* found that volunteers who consumed about four milligrams of vitamin C daily for three years decreased the appearance of wrinkles by 11 per cent.

Tomatoes: Tomatoes can help save your skin. Lycopene, the phytochemical that makes tomatoes red, helps eliminate skin-ageing free radicals caused by ultraviolet rays. The nutrients you get from tomatoes act as excellent protectors from sun damage.

Broccoli: This vegetable is high in antioxidants, including vitamins C and E. The vitamin C in broccoli aids in collagen production and keeps your skin healthy and supple, while vitamin E protects your skin cell membranes and guards against UV radiation damage.

Kidney beans: These legumes help repair cells that have suffered free radical damage. During digestion, protein breaks down into amino acids, the building blocks of cells. Amino acids help to speed the repair and regeneration of skin cells and collagen.

Drink lots and lots of water. For every 15 kilos of body weight, you have to drink 1 litre of water. That's the amount of water your body needs to flush out the toxins in your system and make your skin radiant. A restful sleep is also equally important. I wholly recommend homemade facial packs. The stuff that's available in your kitchen is great for your skin. A very good thing that you can do for your skin is exfoliate. Our skin regenerates and by exfoliating, you are throwing off the dead skin.

I know that men are not going to follow the entire cleansing-toning-moisturising routine. So for them, I recommend three things. First, use a face wash. Then, use a scrub to exfoliate. Men have the advantage of shaving, so they are already exfoliating on a daily basis. But the scrub will remove the dead skin from the forehead and cheeks as well. And the most important thing is to use a sunscreen every time they step out. Indian skins are prone to pigmentation. So a sunscreen will always be beneficial. One of the ways to remove tan from the skin is to cut a potato or tomato, rub it on the skin, keep it for a few minutes and wash it off.

REMOVAL OF FACIAL HAIR

For women, hair around the lips must always be removed. And your eyebrows should also always be shaped. We can all safely say that overgrown eyebrows look extremely unprofessional. Sometimes, when the eyebrows are not done, the most common excuse is: I will shape them when I go to the beauty parlour next. Why do you have to wait to do that? Learn to do it yourself. Once a beautician has shaped them, you can maintain your eyebrows by tweezing new stray hairs every morning. For hair on the rest of your face, you can shave, wax or thread it off, depending on what suits you and what you find least painful. These days, many women use lasers to minimize facial hair growth and permanently remove them.

NAILS

Personal grooming for nails means they should always be clean and shaped. Ideally, your nails should be polished or buffed, or coated with a clear protective coat. Whether nails should be long or short depends on your lifestyle. Regular manicures and pedicures are necessary for both men and women. And you don't always need to go to the beauty parlour for that. There are several instructions online, which help you get a good mani-pedi at home. Dirty finger and toenails are always a rude shock. Please don't neglect your feet. People tend to take care of the body parts that are visible and forget the rest. Don't do that.

HAIR

Your hair should be clean, neat, tidy and devoid of dandruff. Wash it every other day, especially because we live in a hot country. Find a hairstyle that suits the shape of your face. Also consider your lifestyle, when choosing a hairstyle. If you have a fairly busy schedule, a low maintenance hairstyle works better for you. Half your battle is won if you have a good hairstylist. So look for one diligently and you will look great every day. Good hair etiquette also means never scratching your head or combing it in public. If you highlight your hair, be sure to get your roots done regularly.

For men, a neat, trimmed beard or stubble – if you choose to have facial hair – is a must. Scraggy beards are no one's idea of sexy. If the clean-shaven look is what you go for, your sideburns should be trimmed properly. The fuzz on the back of your neck should be shaved regularly. Get a haircut the moment it starts curling under the collar.

Dandruff is unattractive. Use an anti-dandruff shampoo regularly alternating with a regular shampoo. Also, should you use hair oil? I would say yes, only because we have grown up using it. People in western countries don't use it. But since Indians have pretty good hair on the whole, I'm sure hair oil can take some of the credit. Apply oil for about 45 minutes on a clean scalp. People make the mistake of applying it on dirty hair. That clogs the pores. So refrain from doing it. Also, use it only on the scalp because the rest of your hair is dead. When you do that, you end up using more shampoo to get it off and in the process drying your hair even more. Oil is beneficial only on your scalp.

How to be an elegant woman

Put on a bit of makeup every day, so you always look your best and feel confident.

Make sure you remove excessive facial hair on a regular basis.

How to be a well-groomed man

Keep you facial hair as well as the hair on your head trimmed and clean.

Long nails on men is quite simply a turn-off.

2

FITNESS AND NUTRITION

"Take care of your body. It's the only place you have to live."

— Jim Rohn, American businessman

Personal grooming applied to the body means you take care of it. You will feed it good nutritious food, and you will rest it well. Exercise affects your core muscles and that is what gives you good posture. That reason is good enough to engage in exercise.

We all know that regular exercise makes your heart and bones stronger, lowers your risk for chronic disease along with your blood pressure, keeps your weight under control and reduces feelings of anxiety and depression. But do you know why? Exercise increases the blood flow to your brain and releases 'feel-good' hormones that make you feel happier and more relaxed. So while you're boosting your energy levels, oxygen capacity, muscle tone and general fitness, a side benefit is an increase in self-esteem. Just the success of creating an exercise plan and sticking to it allows you to enjoy a sense of achievement and accomplishment. Each kilometre you run, each lap you swim, each kilo you lift in the gym, each calorie you lose shows that when you put your mind to it, you can do something you have never done before. You can challenge yourself and push yourself to the limit. Working out and seeing your body change will definitely help change your attitude towards yourself and even life. When you start feeling good about what you have accomplished your entire perception changes. If you have realistic goals, you will be able to achieve them, and will feel more motivated and confident to keep going and be open to trying new things. This increase in motivation and confidence will also spill over into other areas of your life. Exercise for 20 to 30 minutes every day. Pick an activity you enjoy so you will stick with it and vary what you do to keep boredom away. You can even mix classes, sports and exercise with friends to keep things interesting and your confidence high.

THE LATEST IN WORKOUTS

I am sure by now you are tired of the usual exercise routines and are itching to try something new. Breaking your routine gets you excited about the new thing around the corner and helps you exercise better. Here are some of the latest trends in fitness and exercise that will re-energize you:

Physique 57: This is a barre based workout blended with intervals of cardio, strength training, stretching, and recovery. It is said to create long, lean, supple muscles in the shortest period by targeting certain muscle groups to the point of fatigue. From what I hear, the results are visible almost immediately.

PXT: This is a 60-minute workout mixed with yoga, high-intensity cardio intervals, strength training, plyometrics, calisthenics and core work, to improve overall strength and conditioning. PXT is made up of a yoga warm-up with *surya namaskars* to heat the body, followed by one-minute interval strength training exercises with weights and core ball, followed by a series of challenges and ending with a yoga cool-down sequence.

> Workouts with personal trainers are usually tailored for you to get maximum benefits without overdoing it.

The challenges include several exercises that are done one after another eight times, seven times, six times, etc., working down to one each followed by the cool-down.

Precision running: This is a unique method of treadmill interval training. Instead of mindlessly running on a treadmill, you have constant intervals and inclines to mix it up and help you burn more calories.

SLT: It stands for Strengthen, Lengthen, and Tone. SLT is a mix of Pilates, cardio and strength training, done on a reformer machine. But make sure you're already super fit because SLT is a said to be a challenge for even long-term gym goers.

Aqua cycling: We have all been to at least one spin class and complained about how tough it is later. But here's spinning with a twist. The underwater spin class burns up to 800 calories, enhances blood flow, and combats cellulite in just one workout.

Orange Theory: This intense heart rate based workout can burn up to 1,000 calories an hour, and keep burning for up to 36 hours afterwards. The 60-minute workout centres on a circuit comprising treadmills, rowers and weight training blocks. The name Orange Theory refers to the heart rate zone you are targeting. You wear a monitor to track your performance. If you go above orange, you will burn out. If you stay under it, you aren't pushing hard enough.

Float fit: Float fit is like high intensity interval training but on water. You have to do lunges, push-ups and squats while balancing on an inflatable board. The idea is that because your base is unstable, your muscles have to work even harder to maintain balance, maximising the effect of the class.

PERSONAL TRAINER VS. GOING IT ALONE

While I am not a fitness expert, I exercise regularly, and I know what works for me. So from what I've learned and the experiences of people I know, it is a better idea to have a personal trainer if you visit the gym for your exercise regimen.

Hire one as soon as you sign up for membership. I know it's extra cash that you have to fork out, but remember that the trainer is a professional who understands how the human body works and how to get the best out of it. When you hire a personal trainer right from the beginning, you will become regular with your exercises. You can work with a trainer for three months and then choose to go it alone. Workouts with personal trainers are usually tailored for you to get maximum benefits without overdoing it. They will also support you in fitting in other workouts and activities into your

Every person is different and so the correct balanced diet is likely to vary from person to person. But it will still cover all food groups and will be low in sodium, saturated fats and sugar.

life in a manageable way. What works for one person, may not work for another when it comes to choosing an exercise programme. A personal trainer will develop the most effective programme for you based on your goals. The personal trainer will also ensure that your form and technique is correct right from the beginning. He will make sure you don't drop out because he will call you up when you don't show up. Also, the fact that you've paid money means you are more likely to stick with the regimen, if only to ensure you get your money's worth.

If you have been exercising consistently for several weeks and are not losing weight or reaching your goals, hiring a trainer will be a good choice. A trainer can look at your current programme and eating habits and help you see where you could make changes to create more effective workouts. A trainer can also help you determine if the goals you have set are realistic for you and help you stay motivated to exercise.

We all have areas we would like to work on, and personal trainers can not only tell you realistically what to expect with each workout, but also how to optimize a session to target different muscle groups. They also push your limits. Just when you think you cannot go anymore, you will be told by the trainer to hold for another minute. You do it, and are all the better for it. A personal trainer will keep you from plateauing. He is a great choice if you need some variety in your workouts. A trainer will constantly engage you with new challenges and ways to train. He can bring a fresh perspective and new ideas to challenge both your body and your mind. Even if you just do a few sessions or meet every few weeks, you will find it refreshing to have new workouts and new exercise equipment to try out.

At the gym, for a monthly fee, you will have access to a room full of equipment, classes, and a trainer. Everything you could possibly need will be at this one place. It cannot get easier than that.

A BALANCED DIET

A balanced diet contains foods from all the main food groups in the right proportions to provide your body with everything it needs to remain healthy. It combines the right fats, proteins, carbohydrates, vitamins, minerals and fibre to obtain all of the nutrients you need for good health. Every person is different and so the correct balanced diet is likely to vary from person to person. But it will still cover all food groups and will be low in sodium, saturated fats and sugar.According to the US Departments of Health and Human Services and Agriculture, a diet that is low in saturated and trans fats, cholesterol, added sugar, salt and alcohol should be followed.

The five food groups are:

Vegetables and fruits:　Vegetables have many natural nutrients such as vitamins, minerals, and dietary fibre. Choose vegetables that are in season so you can make the most of it and make sure you have a mix of different colours such as greens (beans, peas and broccoli), reds, oranges or yellows (capsicums, tomatoes, carrots, sweet potato and pumpkin), purples (red cabbage and eggplant), and whites (cauliflower, mushrooms and potatoes). It's better to eat fresh fruit instead of juice, where you are likely to lose dietary fibre. Have generous portions of at least two fruits every day.

Cereals and pulses:　Grains and pulses are high in protein and dietary fibre. They include beans of all sorts, oats, rice, wheat, ragi, jowar, bajra, and breakfast cereals like muesli.

Meat:　Meat is a good source of protein, vitamins and minerals, including iron, zinc and B vitamins. Try to eat lean cuts of meat whenever possible to cut down on fat. Always remember to cook meat thoroughly.

Dairy:　Milk and dairy foods such as cheese and yoghurt are good sources of protein. They also contain calcium, which helps keep your bones healthy.

Fats and oils:　Some fat in the diet is essential, but limit it to only small amounts. It's important to get most of our fat from unsaturated oils and spreads.

Losing weight can only be done with a change in lifestyle. Crash diets will not help you all the time. One of the easiest and sure-fire ways of getting to your target weight is cutting out all refined food. That includes white rice, white bread, *maida* and sugar. Instead of that, you can use brown rice, wholewheat or multigrain bread. Eat breakfast like a king, lunch like a prince and dinner like a pauper. But most of us do it the other way round. Try to change that. Have smaller portions throughout the day. Get up from the table feeling a little hungry. Finish your dinner three hours before you sleep.

WHY GOOD FOOD IS IMPORTANT

Eating healthy isn't always easy, but committing to a healthy diet can be one of the smartest decisions you ever make. Eating well makes you look and feel better, and more confident. What you eat has an impact on your brain, including the parts that regulate your mood. Maintaining stable blood sugar levels through proper nutrition will help you feel better overall. Foods rich in vitamins and minerals, such as fruits, whole grains and vegetables, have been associated with an overall lower risk of depression, as have foods rich in omega-3 fats, such as nuts, salmon and other fatty fish.

True happiness isn't just about the absence of sadness; it also includes general well-being. I frequently hear friends and relatives rave about their increased energy, more stable moods, better sleep and greater ability to focus their thoughts after switching to healthier eating habits.

Eating healthy can also reduce stress. When your body is always stressed, it breaks down protein to prepare for battle, but certain foods have the ability to moderate the body's level of cortisol, the stress hormone. Some studies have found that consuming foods with omega-3 fatty acids and magnesium may help reduce cortisol levels. Eating a protein-rich diet, including fish and dairy, can help replenish protein stores and keep cortisol levels low.

While you are concentrating on what you are eating, don't forget to exercise. Do what you enjoy. If you like jogging, do that. If yoga's your choice of exercise, do that. But do something. When you exercise, you build your self-esteem and confidence because you feel good about yourself. You feel better when you find the clothes you want to wear, not clothes you are trying to fit into.

And that bring us to a very important part of personal grooming – the clothes you wear.

Always remember...
The food you eat is what makes you. Try to eat as healthy as possible.
And for all the times you don't, exercise.

3

ATTIRE

"Clothes make the man. Naked people have little or no influence on society."

— Mark Twain, writer

I was out with a few of my friends on a girls' night out. One of them had invited a couple of her friends to join us directly at the club where entry was only by guest list. After a while, we received a frantic phone call from her friends saying that the bouncer at the door would not let them in. We were confused, as we had clearly put their names on the list. We went to the entrance to bail them out, found the manager and asked him the reason for all that drama. He shot us an incredulous look while pointing out to the two girls waiting at the door dressed in their shortest, tightest dresses, flaunting all their assets. The man looked a little embarrassed, apologized to us, and let them in. While my friend escorted them back into the club, the bouncer confided to me that the real reason the manager didn't let them in was because he mistook them for being 'working girls' who were trying to gate-crash by pretending to be our guests.

This is shocking, yes, but I could not blame the man entirely because he based his judgement, like most people, on his first impression. He could not be further from the truth because I discovered over the course of the night that those two young women turned out to be interesting, intelligent and charming, a far cry from the bimbo get-up that they were in.

My point here is that we do tend to judge people by their appearances. Our clothes make a huge difference to what people think about us – and without us knowing or in ways we couldn't even imagine. People make their assessments in the first few seconds of seeing someone; assessments that go way beyond how well you are dressed and how neat and tidy you might look. That is why I can't stress enough the importance of keeping the visual presentation in sync with who you are and where you are at.

A study of 300 men and women published in the *Journal of Fashion Marketing and Management* showed some of the very subtle ways in which clothing influences all kinds of impressions about us. They looked at images of a man and a woman for just three seconds before making snap judgements about them. In some of the pictures, the man wore a made-to-measure suit. In others, he wore a very similar suit bought from a cheaper store. The differences in the suits were minor and the face of the model was pixelated so that there could be no hidden messages in the facial expressions. After just three seconds, people judged the man in the bespoke suit more favourably. And the judgements were not just about how well dressed he was. They rated him as more confident, successful, flexible and a higher earner in a tailor-made suit than when he wore a cheaper equivalent. Since the model's face in the pictures was blanked out, these impressions must have been formed after quickly eyeing what he was wearing. This shows that our clothes say a great deal about who we are and can signal a great deal of socially important things to others, even if the impression is actually unfounded.

So the next time you are rustling through your closet looking for something to wear, keep a few pointers in mind:

Body type: This should be the basis of how and what you wear. Identify your body type and dress to flatter it. There are a few basic rules to follow for each body type and if you figure out what works best for you, you are less likely to end up making a faux pas. Women of all sizes and shapes can look great by just accepting the pros and cons of their bodies, and learning how to highlight their best features while cleverly covering up their flaws. Indian women tend to have a larger middle or hips. The key to dressing then is to ensure that, that body part is not highlighted. If you wear an A-line dress, it does a good job of covering the stomach as well as the hips. Choosing the right colours also helps. The darker the colour, the better the camouflage. A common mistake people make is wearing a belt in the hope that the stomach will look smaller. In fact, it does the opposite. A belt highlights the area, which is not what you want at all. Wearing a bigger dress or shirt is also a good idea. It hides the fat when the fabric does not cling to the skin. If you are a size 10, try wearing size 12 clothes. I assure you they will look nice on you. This is especially true for men who are sometimes on the verge of bursting out of their tight shirts. Also, vertical strips make you look taller and slimmer, as opposed to horizontal ones that make you look wider. Every designer agrees that this optical illusion is true. Highlight the slimmer body parts by wearing lighter shades and camouflage the larger parts by choosing darker colours. For instance, if you have a slim upper torso, wear a white shirt and choose a black or dark blue skirt for your lower body. The same applies to men as well.

Age: This applies for women of all ages. While teenagers can get away with most fashion mistakes, certain rules apply to them as well. For example, you cannot wear your comfortable Crocs and shredded jeans, however cool they are, as formal attire. Older women should not try to dress like their teenage daughters even if people have said that they look like sisters. They need to have their own more mature style and elegant way of dressing.

> Invest in timeless pieces, and you will never be at a loss for what to wear whenever the special occasion comes calling.

Less is always more: This is a cardinal rule that applies to more than dressing. But that doesn't mean that you take this literally and show up in something skimpy. Even if you have the body to carry off the shortest and tightest of clothes, you do not have to flaunt everything all at once. If you do want to show off a little cleavage, try to keep the skirt length a little longer. Ideally, pick one aspect of your appearance you want to flaunt, for example, toned legs or a trim waistline, and highlight just that.

Dress for the occasion: Always bear in mind where you are heading to, when you are choosing your outfit. If you are unsure about the dress code, you can always check with your host so that you don't stand out like a sore thumb. The safest option would be to dress elegantly and in something that you are comfortable and can carry off confidently.

Fashion faux pas: Fashion trends are ever evolving and as tempting as it is to follow them all, sometimes it is a better idea to avoid them. You can always incorporate a few of the current trends such as the colour of the season or a particular style of sleeve or even a popular print like florals or geometrical or an Aztec print. You can be a fashionista without being a fashion victim.

Invest in timeless pieces, and you will never be at a loss for what to wear whenever the special occasion comes calling.

For women

Black trousers:　A sleek pair of black trousers with a flattering fit is one of the few wardrobe staples that you can wear with just about anything else in your cupboard.

Black suit:　In the corporate world, a perfectly tailored black suit is foolproof. But it has appeal beyond the workplace: when you show up anywhere dressed in a well-fitted jacket and skirt, you look proper, polished, and modern. That's why it is important to invest in the best-constructed suit you can afford.

Little black dress:　Every woman knows she should have a little black dress, but invest in one that's special. Look for a dress with a special detail – an interesting sleeve, an embellished belt – that makes it unique. And of course, it has to fit you just right.

Classic bag:　A smart, well-matched handbag will complement the outfit.

Day dress:　This one should be feminine, flattering and functional.

White T-shirt:　The white shirt is very versatile, so find a version in a great cut that you can wear with everything from jeans to pants and skirts.

Heels:　Every woman needs a pair of statement heels. Whether you opt for vibrant colour, a statement print, or detailing, this pair should be the one you throw on with everything from jeans to your evening dresses.

Dark jeans:　A well-fitted pair of jeans goes well with T-shirts, blouses, business blazers as well as ballerina flats.

For men

Suit: No man can be without a black or a navy suit. Navy blue is a masculine colour that works with a range of shirt and tie colours. The right navy suit can work for a whole range of occasions from dressy to informal.

Formal trousers: A well-fitted pair of trousers can do wonders for a man's look. Have one each in black, brown, grey and navy blue.

Jeans: Dark blue jeans, which can be worn even for a brunch or luncheon, can be paired with a blazer and still look elegant, or dressed down with pullover and shirt and still look classy.

White shirt: A crisp white shirt is a non-negotiable part of a man's closet. You must have a white shirt.

Black shoes: Pair these with black socks.

T-shirts: T-shirts in black, white and grey should suffice. T-shirts in these basic colours makes them more versatile.

The most important thing to remember is to look the part. I know a gentleman who is the CEO of a company. He had gone with his son for a conference. Because of the hot weather there, the father was wearing shorts, but the son was impeccably dressed in a fitted suit. Everyone flocked to the son even though he was not the boss. The same surname meant people didn't know who was who. He had to correct everyone, saying that his father was whom they wanted to talk to. This is the perfect example of why dressing well all the time is only a good thing. This reinforces the importance of looking the part. If there is a dress code, you have to adhere to it in the corporate world.

First, make sure your clothes are in good condition. Choose colours that suit you. If you have dark skin, don't wear drab colours like brown and grey. They do nothing for your look. Wear a clean, crisp shirt. You can keep the top button open. Anything more and you will look completely out of place. Your shoes should match your socks. Don't wear casual moccasins or sneakers for a night out. Invest in a good pair of leather shoes. Keep them polished always. A nice belt with a slightly bigger buckle than what you wear during the day is a good idea. Depending on the weather, men can accessorize with a scarf, muffler or a well-fitted jacket.

GETTING JEWELRY RIGHT

A tasteful piece of jewelry can transform an ordinary outfit into a stylish number. Jewelry is not gender-specific. However, the time, place and occasion should determine the jewelry that a man wears. According to one of my favourite jewelers, "Your jewelry should make a strong and bold impression." He emphasizes that the vintage look is very in. Trends range from costume jewelry and chunky boho to casual ethnic pieces and luxury estate jewelry. Keep these few things in mind when you are choosing your jewelry for the day.

- Long dangling earrings look good on a bare neck.
- Go for subtle, small pieces in the day and heavier pieces in the evening.
- At a business meeting, go for minimalism: small earrings with a tiny pendant, or a couple of pearl strands.
- Long necklaces and chunky rings are fine for cocktail parties.
- Save all the heavy sparkling ornaments for grand occasions, like weddings.
- Long chains of semi-precious stones and crystals, along with several bracelets, can be worn at any time.
- Keep the focus on just one piece of jewelry– be it a grand necklace, vintage rings or chandelier earrings.
- The jewelry needn't always be colour-coordinated.

Finally, determine what suits your personality and wear it with confidence. Epictetus got it right when he said, "Know, first, who you are; and then adorn yourself accordingly."

How to be an elegant woman

Invest in a day dress, a well-fitting suit, a chic handbag, heels and dark jeans.
A couple of pieces of jewelry can change your look completely. Choose something that suits you.

How to be a well-dressed man

Dress for your age.
You should always have a suit, crisp white shirt, your go-to T-shirts and black shoes in your wardrobe.

CORPORATE DRESSING

Corporate dressing is a powerful tool in the office space. How you dress to work is an indication of your personality and, if carried off confidently, it instantly elevates your self-esteem and portrays you as a poised, polished and professional person. In today's globalized corporate working environment, if you want to make an impact you will have to dress sharp. Most conventional organisations such as banks, financial institutions and the hospitality industry have very demarcated rules for dressing for both men and women. In the world of media, advertising, film and the more creative fields, the rules are a little relaxed, allowing a more flexible approach to dressing. However, I firmly believe that if you want the business or are selling a service, you definitely need to look like a thorough professional to be taken seriously. For example, I am selling this etiquette book, so

> Treat your corporate clothing as an investment and make wise choices. Just an expensive brand isn't good enough. Your clothes should be well- fitted and in good condition.

you will never see me shabbily dressed. Even if it's to go to the market below my house, I will have a clean dress on and basic hair done. I will never be seen scruffy. Similarly, if you are in the fitness industry, you had better have a fabulous body. If you are a dietician, you have no choice but to be fit. If you are an actor, you have to look beautiful and well kept. There's a big gym near my house and the woman at the counter – the first person anyone entering the gym sees – is severely overweight. I went there to sign up, but left thinking there's no way I want to exercise there. If I am going to a hair salon and the person at the counter has dandruff, I will turn around immediately. It's all about making the right impression. Friends of mine were invited for dinner at the house of someone they didn't know. When an impeccably dressed gentleman opened the door, they thought he was the host and thanked him for inviting them. Turns out, he was the butler.

Treat your corporate clothing as an investment and make wise choices. Just an expensive brand isn't good enough. Your clothes should be well-fitted and in good condition. By well-fitted, I do not mean body-hugging but comfortable enough to work in all day. Make sure you buy classic, timeless styles that flatter your body type, are comfortable and have quality workmanship. That way they would probably last you longer.

A study on the three Vs of first impressions show that 55 per cent is 'Visual' (based on the way you look), 7 per cent is 'Verbal' (a few words that you speak) and 38 per cent is 'Voice' (the way you sound). A well-groomed and suitably attired person obtains instant respect, whereas a flippant person, who is inappropriately dressed, kills by their appearance any desire to conduct business dealings with them. In business matters, your appearance should convey the right message. In order to look relatively up-to-date, fashion magazines can be of great help. A little later, I have mentioned the tips for business dressing for men and women separately and in depth, but here are some things that apply to both:

- Clothes should be clean, well ironed and in good shape, not frayed.

- Business colours would include black, navy blue, brown, grey or beige teamed with pastels, flat colours or pinstripes. Steer clear from loud prints, Lycra and metallic embellishments.

- The classic, well-tailored suit as a business formal is an all-time winner. The jacket can be single or double-breasted. A single-breasted jacket may be worn buttoned or teamed with a collared shirt and can be left unbuttoned. The double-breasted jacket is always worn buttoned. The length of the jacket should be no longer than the top of your wrist if you are standing with your arms straight down. The length of the trouser should be one-and-a-half inch from the floor to the back of your heel. There should be just one neat iron crease line on the pant. Shirts should be neatly tucked in. Shirt buttons, the belt and the fly should all be in one straight line.

- Undergarments should be invisible.

- As a rule, shoes, bags and belts should always be coordinated.
- Closed shoes are generally worn with a business suit. However, open-toed sandals are also acceptable.
- Skirts should be no shorter than four inches above the knee.
- Visible tattoos and body piercing are taboo in the business world.

The rules are slightly different for men and women about corporate dressing. And while the men have less room to explore their fashionable side in the business world, us women can make it a little less drab. Here are a few things women need to keep in mind:

1. The classic suit should be a wardrobe staple. Jackets can be worn with either pants or skirts. The length of the skirt should be no shorter than four inches above the knee. If you want a slightly different look, opt for a sleeveless dress with a jacket or even a shirtdress.

2. Colours play a very important role. The traditionally accepted hues would be blacks, creams, beige, and navy blue. But you can play with some pastels as well and pair them with one of the more traditional colours. Avoid loud colourful prints, as they can bedistracting.

3. When conducting business, you do not want anything taking away from the matter at hand. Accessories such as shoes, belts and bags must be from the same colour family.

4. Shirts or tops worn under your jackets or with pants or skirts need to have sleeves, in case you need to take your jacket off. Steer clear of sleeveless, transparent or cleavage exposing tops. You could opt for stripes or a very small print for your shirts. Just leave one or two buttons of your shirt open at most. Showing off your chest is repulsive at work.

5. Keep in mind the fabric you choose. Even though linen is the best thing to wear in our climate, it may not be the best option, as you would look terribly unkempt at the end of the day with all the wrinkling. A cotton or linen blend would be a better option, as they would keep you comfortable all day while staying in better shape.

6. Wear minimum jewellery at work. It should be small and subtle and not the focus of your attire. That also includes

engagements rings. Limit yourself to one or two small pieces of jewellery in a classic style. Again, the objective is that the focus should be on your work. Pearls work the best and are always a timeless and elegant choice. The same rule applies for watches – don't wear flashy oversized dials or glittery plastic straps. Straps need to be of leather preferably or a metal bracelet type. Belts and shoes also need to be leather.

7. It is mandatory to wear minimum makeup. But keep it subtle. As I mentioned earlier, you need to put on a basic compact and a lipstick to complete that professional look. Nail colours should be matte. Avoid frosted nail colours.

8. Low necklines are unacceptable and send out wrong signals. In some offices, sleeveless blouses are also frowned upon.

Men though have much fewer options in this regard. The corporate or power suit is the most widely accepted attire. You can choose from the single- or double-breasted jacket, though the single-breasted jacket is definitely more widely used.

1. Suits could be in solid colours or pinstripes. The colours again would mostly be the same except for the creams and lighter beiges. Brown would be a better option for men and to break the monotony, you could experiment with greys. You could opt for a check jacket on plain trousers but make sure it's a very small check pattern.

2. Shirts under solid coloured suits can be pinstriped or plain and in a contrasting colour. You can also pick pastel coloured shirts or white, creams and beige to wear under a dark solid coloured suit.

3. Prints for shirts would include stripes, small checks or self embossed.

4. The tie, of course, is mandatory. Again no loud colours, floral prints or cartoon characters, no matter how much you love them. Stripes and small prints are acceptable if they are not too loud. A subtle self embossed pattern works well too. Cuff links add a nice touch to the corporate suit but that is optional.

5. Belts and shoes need to be from the same colour family and always made of leather. Shoes need to be well-maintained

and not scruffy looking, and highly polished. Avoid large or flashy belt buckles. Watches and watch straps need to be elegant and simple in plain blacks or browns with simple white/gold/silver dials.

> Socks should always match the colour of your trousers or shoes and not the shirt. White sports socks only belong with sports shoes and should never be worn on formal attire.

6. When wearing a double-breasted suit, it is mandatory to keep the jacket buttoned while standing. However, while sitting, the lowest button of the jacket can be undone for comfort. The jacket of a single-breasted suit can be either buttoned or unbuttoned, when standing or sitting.

7. Lastly, a very important and widely believed misconception is that socks should match your shirt. That could not be more wrong. Socks should always match the colour of your trousers or shoes and not the shirt. White sports socks only belong with sports shoes and should never be worn on formal attire.

FRIDAY DRESSING

This is what I like to call corporate casual. But you can't take that too literally and turn up in your Bermudas with pop art T-shirts and flip flops. Chic casual attire has been looked upon as a more relaxed corporate dress code and hence the most misunderstood dress code. As long as you are in the workspace, conducting business, the professional avatar has to be maintained, just toned down as you near the weekend.

For men

1. You can choose between either jeans or khakis instead of the formal suit. Your jeans would have to be in dark blue with no frayed or torn edges. You could pair these with collared T-shirts and moccasins. Round necked T-shirts are not acceptable. They would of course, have to be in solid colours with no graphic prints or loud messages. You could even throw on a light linen or sports jacket in case you need

to run into a meeting.

2. The shoes, belt and accessories all follow the same rules as with the more formal look.

For women

1. Women's options are the same – either a pair of dark denims or khakis with a collared T-shirt and a light jacket. You can also opt for a casual shirtdress in a light cotton fabric. The no-sleeveless rule still applies though.

2. When it comes to shoes, you could skip the heels and chose a pair of moccasins or ballerinas as long as they have a slightly formal look. Strappy glittery sandals or metallic flip-flops belong only on the beach.

Throughout the book, we talk much about first impressions being the most lasting ones. But unfortunately, it is human nature to focus on the negative aspects of a person's appearance and not with what is good and right. So ensure you smell good 24/7, your attire is appropriate for the occasion, makeup in place, hair neatly coiffered, manicured nails and throw in poise, posture and a pleasant facial expression and you cannot go wrong making that perfect first impression.

How to be an elegant woman

Choose fabrics that suit the Indian weather. So stay away from synthetic ones.

Keep your accessories to the minimum because you don't want the attention to be taken away from you and your work. Make sure they are from the same colour family.

Your innerwear should never be visible.

You can wear open flats or ballerinas on Fridays.

How to be a well-dressed man

Belts and shoes need to be from the same colour family and always made of leather.

Always wear a tie to work if you are in a very formal office. Make sure they are not loud and are in muted colours.

Your suits should be in solid colours or sometimes pinstripes.

ENTERTAINING

1

HOW TO BE THE PERFECT PARTY HOST OR GUEST

"I like large parties. They are so intimate. At small parties, there isn't any privacy."

– F. Scott Fitzgerald, writer

This was just the invitation that we were dreading. My husband and I had been invited to a party we didn't want to attend. But we had committed to showing up so there was no way out of it. As much as we love our friends, sometimes we loathe, almost fear, attending parties at their home. People often invite more guests than they can accommodate, it's often hot because too many people have been crammed into the room and we have to watch out for the constant pushing and shoving for fear of spilling drinks all over our clothes. The last time I went to such a party, the music was too loud, the lights were too dim to see what I was eating, and worst of all, the food ran out. This is no party. It was a punishing evening that had to be endured for the sake of a good friendship.

Hosting intimate parties for close friends and family at home may seem like a cakewalk, but we are not talking about being huddled around the television with a couple of beers and ordering takeaway. Entertaining in your house involves plenty of careful planning and coordination. The objective is to make the event a super success and make your guests eagerly await your next invitation. Some people believe that serving the most expensive alcohol and hiring the best caterer in town is good enough. But that doesn't always do the trick. Many other factors need to be brought into consideration to ensure a relaxed, enjoyable evening for your guests. The hallmark of a well-organized successful dinner party is when the host has enjoyed it as much as the guests.

Let's start with a few most imperative pointers that you must consider when hosting a party at home:

CHOOSE A THEME

While this isn't always necessary, everyone almost always enjoys a themed party. It gives guests a chance to think a bit more about the party and their attire for the evening. It will also set your party apart from the others that you and your friends have attended. There's no better icebreaker than a theme.

Having a theme will give you direction for what kind of decorations and invitations to purchase. It will also make it easier to decide what games to play, if any, and what food to serve. You can choose from thousands of themes. It can be seasonal, or something you and your friends will all enjoy. I have noticed though that everyone loves a costume party. If your theme can include costumes, then do it in any way possible, no matter how small. Almost any themed party could easily turn into a costume party with a little effort. If you want your party to be a memorable one, insist that your guests wear costumes based on the theme you have chosen. The more creative everyone is, the better the costumes will get.

The most important thing is to have fun with it. Be creative and give the party your own stamp and touch. Pinterest is a great source for all things creative. You will get plenty of planning ideas from there. Make an impact with your decor. It is not necessarily about quantity as much as it is about quality and thoughtfulness. When it comes to invitations, Facebook isn't the way to go about it. Facebook invitations don't count, neither do SMSes or WhatsApp messages. You love receiving snail mail, don't you? So why not courier your invitations? That will give your party a very personal touch. Ask around for some local quirky designers who can make you a special invite that can never be replicated. If that seems like too much of a hassle, nothing beats personally calling everyone up and inviting them.

> The hallmark of a well-organized successful dinner party is when the host has enjoyed it as much as the guests.

Finally, once everyone has arrived and is having a blast at your unique themed party, don't forget to take lots of pictures. If the budget permits, hire a photographer with a Polaroid camera so your friends can get their pictures immediately. That way, no one will be stuck to their phones and will make the most of their time at your home.

MAKE A GUEST LIST

This is the most crucial aspect. Always remember to get the right mix of people together. Your guests should complement each other. A talented host will have a knack for assembling the right people together. Keep a few extra names handy in case of dropouts. Having empty seats at the table is not the best indication of your social skills.

INVITATIONS

Your invitations will set the tone for your party. (And they are invitations, by the way, not invites.) An invitation by phone call or text suggests an informal get together. An embossed card sent four to six weeks in advance suggests something much grander altogether. These days, it is acceptable to invite guests via email. The thing to remember is that everyone must be invited in the same way at the same time. You cannot invite closer friends with a formal card and acquaintances

Strike the right balance with sweet, spicy and savoury dishes so that there is something on the menu to suit everyone's palate.

with a phone call or online message. That's just tacky and doesn't sit well with your generous personality. Last-minute invitations are extremely rude and rarely accepted. If you do send out a text or online invitation, follow that up with a phone call. That will be a lovely gesture on your part.

The invitation must say who is throwing the party, what kind it is, and when and where it is happening. Be sure to state the day, date, time and address very clearly so there's no confusion. Avoid mentioning the date as the following Sunday, for instance. Be more specific like Sunday, September 18. I have had people show up at my doorstep on the wrong day and me having to receive them in my bathrobe with only an uncomfortable expression for company. Not to mention how embarrassed your guest would feel as well.

RESPONDEZ S'IL VOUS PLAIT

Commonly known in English as RSVP, you must insist that your guests confirm their presence or absence well ahead in time. This is very important when figuring out how much food and beverage will be required.

PLAN THE MENU

Keep in mind your guests' food and drink preferences when setting the menu. Also, it is a good idea to inquire about food allergies. Do not try to be too experimental, as most people generally prefer to stick to tried-and-tested dishes. Pay close attention to the table setting and focus on presentation. Candles or flowers add a lovely touch to decorating the table, but keep it simple. Ensure that the crockery, cutlery, glassware and table linen are clean and well matched.

Food should be served hot and should look appetizing. Instruct servers to serve from the left and clear from the right hand side of the guests. Strike the right balance with sweet, spicy and savoury dishes so that there is something on the menu to suit everyone's palate. Ensure the bar is well stocked with the wine and champagne stored at the right temperature. Make sure it's a substantial meal so that your guests don't go home and raid their own refrigerators. Just because you are on a diet does not mean everyone else has to follow suit.

WELCOMING THE GUESTS

By this time, I hope that you are ready when you said the evening would begin. It sounds simple, but it's a common mistake. One of the easiest mistakes hosts make is that they are not ready on time. The table should be laid out, the air conditioning turned on, and the food and drinks ready at least half an hour before guests arrive.

As a good party host, your job is to ensure your guests feel thoroughly at home. Go out of your way to introduce the guests to one another, especially to those they may not know. And keep an eye on what's happening at all times, making sure that everyone has someone to talk to and that the mixing and mingling never stops. Good manners are about making the other person feel good, so make your small talk all about them and not at all about you.

Welcome your guests at the door so you can greet people and usher them in. Once enough guests have arrived, move to the middle of the room. Drawing in the new arrivals and introduce them to the chatty friendly sort of friend whose company they might enjoy. When it's time to wrap up, set yourself up close to the door again so people can say goodbye easily.

And, whether you're a host or a guest, the most important rule to remember when it comes to good manners: never look over someone's shoulder for someone more interesting to talk to. It's better to feign a couple of minutes of rapt attention and then excuse yourself, either using the 'fill the glass' trick or explaining that you need to go to the toilet.

PLAN THE GUEST SEATING

If you are having a sit-down meal, the rule is to seat the women and the men alternatively. Also don't be afraid to break up the regular gang that sticks together and try to mix the new guests with the regulars. Traditionally, as the host, you sit at the head of the table with your spouse seated exactly opposite at the other end. If there is a special guest in whose honour the dinner is being hosted, that person would be seated on your right. To make the entire exercise easier, you can just plan in advance and place little name cards at each place setting so that your guests do not have to play a game of musical chairs at the dinner table.

But if it's an informal party, a buffet will do just fine. That will give your guests the opportunity to mingle with everyone present and not just the person they are seated next to.

CREATE THE RIGHT AMBIENCE

The right atmosphere means that your guests have an enjoyable evening. Avoid harsh, direct lights and opt for enough lighting that would enable your guests to see each other and their food. Avoid using anything that emits a strong fragrance. Also, make sure that floral table arrangements or other such things do not get in the way of passing things around on the table and turn into a potential fire hazard.

If you have a small table, putting one centrepiece is a better option. Again, it should not be overpowering and guests should be able to see each other across the table without having to crane their necks over it. If you have background music playing, it should only be faintly audible so that people do not have to shout above it. Arrange your furniture in a way that allows guests to circulate and join various groups. The air conditioning should be set at the right temperature and if the room appears crowded drop the temperature by a couple of degrees. There should be an open area for the smokers.

Before inviting people over, make sure you are well equipped to entertain at home as regards space, household help, etc. Dinner parties work best for smaller groups of people. If your home is big enough and can comfortably accommodate larger numbers, you can opt to have a buffet style dinner but still make sure that there is enough seating and people are not stepping on each other's toes with food plates in their hands.

A good host will always have one eye on their guests making sure their glasses are refilled, encouraging the loners to mingle by introducing them to like-minded people whose company they might enjoy. Simultaneously, take the time to enjoy your own party without looked frazzled. A relaxed host is a true testament of a well-planned and well executed event. Last, don't worry about any of it too much. You set the tone: if you are relaxed, your guests will be.

Always remember...

Set a theme for the party and inform your guests much in advance so they have ample time to get ready.

The menu should be in accordance with the theme, if you are going with one, or something you know most of your guests will enjoy.

Be there at the door to welcome all your guests and encourage them to mingle with like-minded people. Choose the lighting well, so it sets a good tone for the party.

2

HOW TO BE A GUEST AT A PARTY

"When you're the most happening person at the party, it's time to leave."

— Kelly Cutrone, Hollywood publicist

Now the tables are turned, and you are a guest. Guest-tiquette, as I like to call it, is equally important. In Indian culture, the guest is equated to the gods. That's why it's even more important to be a pleasure to your host.

If you accept, show up. Try to arrive on time with maybe a delay of 15 or 20 minutes at the most. People love to make a fashionably late entrance, but that would sometimes inconvenience your host about serving dinner, etc. If you are bringing along an extra person, don't just show up with them. It's likely that the host will be fine with your guest, but that's not a decision you get to make. 'The more the merrier' is usually true, but it is not your call as a guest. A good host is going to welcome the uninvited guest in and make them feel just as comfortable. Give the host a heads-up and ask if it would be fine to bring them along.

When you are invited, inquire about the occasion or reason for the celebration. Depending on whether it is a birthday, housewarming or just a casual dinner party, you could figure out an appropriate gift for your host.

AVOID A FASHION FAUX PAS

It is always prudent to make discreet inquiries about the guest list and dress code. You do not want to show up in an overtly sexy outfit at a family event where everyone else is elegantly dressed in traditional wear and spend the evening feeling self-conscious. That does not mean that you cannot wear a dress… of course you can, but an appropriate one.

At the party, all that is expected of you is that you mix and mingle. Socially, we usually greet people with a hug and a couple of air kisses. But sometimes, people don't understand the concept of personal space and hug you too tightly. And don't even get me started on the

> Do not stay on until the end, no matter how much fun you are having. Try to leave with everyone else. Unless you are closely related to the host, you should not be the last to leave.

dodging that happens while air-kissing. People get confused as to which cheek to offer first and end up kissing on the mouth. This is something I have encountered a lot recently. The best way to handle such a situation is to just laugh it off. Unless that person is a known creep, I am sure they didn't mean to kiss you on the mouth. There's no set way to air kiss. But what I do is I give a clear indication that I'll be offering my right cheek. I can do this when I am standing at a comfortable distance so the person can see me approaching. If I stand too close, the person won't be able to know which cheek I'm offering.

DRINK WITHIN YOUR LIMITS

If you are one of the first ones to arrive, do offer to help get people drinks, hand round pre-dinner nibbles or get the door. Have a couple of drinks, but no more. Drink within your capacity so that you are not an embarrassment to your host. Years ago, I was invited for a sit-down dinner in England. We were all having a lovely time even though some of the guests were on their way to getting drunk. However, one of them was so drunk that he dunked his hand in a bowl of chicken gravy, fished out a leg and started eating it. We were all so horrified to witness that. We were embarrassed for him and for us at that moment. Stay abreast of current events, movies, restaurants, etc., so that you can keep the conversation flowing smoothly.

I have often been asked if a woman should remain seated or should stand up, when introduced to someone at a party. The answer depends on what kind of party it is. At a business do, it would be correct to rise and greet whomever you are introduced to regardless of their age. Here, the action is not gender specific. However, at any other time, it is fine to remain seated and extend your hand in a handshake.

Being polite and respectful at a party is a given. Once, at another party, my husband and I attended, a couple got into a very serious fight. It started out just verbally and soon escalated to them screaming at each other in front of all of us. And at one point, one of them threw a glass at the other, and the other person did the same. We were all so shocked by the behaviour that we couldn't react at all for a few moments. It was quite an unnerving situation. The best way to diffuse this heated moment is to separate the warring sides. Take charge, take one of them to a room, and ask your friends to take the other person to another room. The distance will calm both of them down and will surely not escalate.

Do not stay on until the end, no matter how much fun you are having. Try to leave with everyone else. Unless you are closely related to the host, you should not be the last to leave. If anyone tells you that you are 'the life and soul of the party', it's time to go home. You have definitely gone too far. Your host has probably had a long and tiring day and may want to wind up at an earthly hour.

Say thank you when you leave, of course. Tell the host what you loved about the evening. Maybe you loved the company or the food was excellent. Tell that to the host. An even better thing to do is to send a note or a message the next day.

Always remember...

Since guests are treated as gods in our country, make sure you never take advantage of your host. Don't make ludicrous demands, and always say thank you for everything your host does for you.

Do not spoil the fun for yourself and others by drinking more alcohol than you can handle.

Even if you've not been informed of any dress code, it's best to inquire about what everyone else is wearing so you don't stand out negatively.

Mingle with everyone at the party and don't stick to just your friends.

3

GETTING OVER THAT OOPS MOMENT

"It is easy to decide on what is wrong to wear to a party, such as deep-sea diving equipment or a pair of large pillows, but deciding what is right is much trickier."

— Lemony Snicket, *The Slippery Slope*

You are in a group, within obvious hearing distance of a set of people, and you belch, pass wind, or send out a spray of spit. You are at a sit-down dinner or even holding a plate at a buffet line, and you spill food on your clothes. You introduce two people only to realize you have said one of the names wrong or mispronounced them. Or worse, you begin to introduce two people and suddenly realize you just can't remember one of the names. No matter what, all hope is not lost. You cannot leave, obviously, but you have to display grace under pressure. You can gather yourself, your composure and complete your social commitment as you intended to.

Even the most blessed and impeccably mannered have, at some time or other, had the misfortune of committing a faux pas — hoping that the floor would open up and swallow them. But we're not robots programmed to perform with total precision, but human beings with shortcomings. So, we're bound to fail at times. If you have unfortunately lost control or have made audible embarrassing sounds, don't get flustered. Excuse yourself and calmly get on with the business at hand. The others in the group, however, must also say, "It happens to the best of us," and continue without missing a beat.

On the other hand, if you drool or drip on your designer outfit at that fancy dinner, again, quietly excuse yourself and retire to the washroom to wash the stain. Soda is the quickest and most effective stain remover I can recommend. Refrain from trying to scrub the stain at the table or in public. Don't continually verbalize your dismay or your disappointment either. You will end up embarrassing yourself and those around you. Not to mention boring them as well.

> When you have committed a faux pas, don't apologize profusely or draw unnecessary attention to yourself and the blunder.

When introducing your guests, if you mispronounce a name or, worse still, are momentarily struck with temporary amnesia, don't panic. Charmingly smile, apologize sweetly with an 'I'm awfully sorry' and quickly correct yourself. Get it right the next time though. The person whose name you have mispronounced or forgotten would or should normally, supply the correct name and pronunciation — without making a big deal about it.

When you have committed a faux pas, don't apologize profusely or draw unnecessary attention to yourself and the blunder. Doing so or offering an explanation, which you are tempted to do or it is often a reflex action, will ensure that you and your gaffe remain etched in their memories forever.

TALKING TO SOMEONE YOU DON'T WANT TO

At a party, you meet all sorts of people. Some you will like and some will test your patience. A friend once told me about one man she would always meet at parties. They always had someone in common and would hence bump into each other almost every week. "He was a colossal bore, and would just drone on and on about whatever topic caught his fancy at that time. Believe me when I tell you that once he spoke at least half an hour about the breeding habits of the housefly. I didn't know how to get myself away from him without being rude." Well, here's the advice I gave her.

Take charge of the conversation: Find something interesting in what they are saying and begin talking about it. They will hopefully take your hint and let you speak. Steer the conversation in a direction that interests you.

Change the topic: Knowing how to change the subject is an important skill, especially if you cannot abandon the conversation. Honesty is the best policy: "I'm sorry to change the subject, but I'm interested in hearing what you think about..." should do it.

When all else fails, say goodbye: But if nothing else works and you can't stand to be around this person any more, just tell them you need to talk to a friend you haven't seen in a while and say your goodbyes.

WHEN SOMEONE SPILLS A DRINK ON YOU

This is a common occurrence at parties and is almost always unintentional. Be gracious and clean up with a towel there and then more thoroughly in the restroom. Don't scream or curse at the other person because first, that is uncalled for and second, will only make the situation even more embarrassing for the both of you. Make the best of the situation, smile and put the spiller at ease because they are probably more embarrassed than you at ruining your clothes.

When someone's partner hits on you: Now this is an awkward social situation. If you find yourself at the receiving end of some unwanted interest, keep their spouse as the topic of conversation. That way he or she won't forget they are coupled up and this behaviour is unbecoming of them. Of course, if they don't get the hint and persist, feel free to just shut them down. And please don't feel uncomfortable or guilty while doing it. This is not your fault at all.

When a drunken person acts out: The first thing to remember is to stay calm. There's no point screaming, shouting or reprimanding the drunken person because it won't make a difference. Then, move them away from everyone so you can nip the scene in the bud. Take them to a room where they can sleep it off. Take a trusted person's help if you need. You can also get someone to drive them home. But under no circumstances should you let them drive home. Take away their car keys so that there is one less intoxicated person on the streets. Never use physical strength to persuade them to do what you want. He or she is an impaired guest and is likely to become angry and the situation could escalate into a fight.

Always remember...

It's not a sin or an insult to forget someone's name. Just apologize and ask them for it.

Handle a drunken guest with empathy and patience.

Don't shout if someone spills a drink or drops food on you by mistake. Just say it's not a problem and walk towards the restroom to clean it up.

4

RESTAURANT ETIQUETTE

"Nothing is less important than which fork you use. Etiquette is the science of living. It embraces everything. It is ethics. It is honour."

– Emily Post, author

We decided to celebrate my daughter's graduation by taking her to her favourite restaurant for a family dinner. As it was the weekend, the place was naturally packed, but we were shown to our reserved table. Seated beside us was a group of young people who seemed to be having a birthday celebration and were in rather high spirits. After ordering our drinks, we tried very hard to have a conversation, but it was getting increasingly impossible because the group next to us was getting louder and more boisterous. Added to that, the ribald jokes and foul language didn't do much to help our appetites. My husband then requested the maître d' if we could get another table. But that was not an option, as they were fully booked. We then proceeded to request the manager to ask the group to keep it down which he did, but that only worked for about five minutes after which it was the same story. My daughter was now feeling embarrassed because we were 'making a scene' and was convinced that the other table was giving us dirty looks, all the while sniggering and making jokes at our expense. Least to say, it wasn't the lovely family dinner we had planned.

> Dining etiquette rules apply before you even take your seat and continue after you excuse yourself from the table.

I am not playing spoilsport here and I understand that when a bunch of friends get together, they want to have a good time. But you do not have to do it at the cost of making everyone around you bear the brunt of loud, brash behaviour. People generally come to restaurants to enjoy the food, ambience as well as the company of family and friends. If you want to be loud and rambunctious, do so by all means, but pick a more apt venue like a lounge bar or a club or maybe a private dining area. Dining etiquette rules apply before you even take your seat and continue after you excuse yourself from the table.

I was at a restaurant recently, and could not help but notice a group of four young women walk in, nonchalantly ask a passing waiter if they could take the first table and then proceed to sit there. When the maître d' came by in a few minutes and said another group had been waiting for that table, they seemed to take great offence. It took many apologies and much persuasion on the maître d's part to relocate them. Was this impolite behaviour on the restaurant's part? Or is it appropriate to wait only for a maître d' to seat you, no matter how big or small the restaurant, or whether or not you have a reservation? What is the best way to conduct yourself at a restaurant – from the time you enter, seat yourself, order and pay?

It's absolutely inappropriate for the maître d' to dislodge a customer who has been seated by a steward in his absence. Having created a blunder, the restaurant would have to bear the consequences. However, if the group has seated themselves, it would be within his right to request them to move. If the restaurant has maître d' seating, it is solely the maître d's responsibility to seat customers according to prior reservations. The reservation register is maintained, with specific table requests, for the precise purpose of avoiding any faux pas. Delegating a reliever while he's on a break would avoid any embarrassments.

> If you are in a large group, stick to talking to the people in close proximity and avoid shouting across the table or discussing inappropriate topics with the person seated across.

That is why while visiting a restaurant, first please do make a reservation, especially if you plan to go on the weekend or a busy night. Don't arrive there and then expect to be seated out of turn. I regularly see people trying to drop names, cajole or bribe the manager to get the table as soon as possible. It is far easier to just make a reservation in advance.

In the event of a cancellation, it would be nice to inform the restaurant so that they do not hold the table waiting for you to show up. Most restaurants nowadays will call to reconfirm bookings. On a very busy night, if they have many people waiting they might be inclined to give your table away so try to get there on time.

GETTING SEATED

Protocol demands that you always wait to be seated. Be prepared to be shunted if you take the liberty of plonking yourself at any table. If you have table preferences, take the time to make a reservation. The lady must follow the maître d' to the table ahead of the gentleman and be seated first. Immediately place your napkin on your lap.

ORDERING

When placing your order, read the name correctly from the menu. If you find, say, a French name unpronounceable, just smile at the maître d' and take assistance. If you are unsure about what wine to order, ask for help. There's no shame in doing that.

DURING THE MEAL

When eating, sit up straight. Bring the food up to your mouth. Never stoop towards the food. If you spill, don't make a scene. Excuse yourself and repair the damage in the washroom. Should you spill on the tablecloth, ignore it. Proper posture at the table is important. Sit upright with arms near the body and elbows off the table. Never pick your teeth at the table, spit a piece of bad food or gristle into your napkin. Neither should you speak with food in your mouth, lest you spray it on others. Make pleasant table talk, steering clear off controversial topics. If you are in a large group, stick to talking to the people in close proximity and avoid shouting across the table or discussing inappropriate topics with the person seated across. Your fellow diners may be having their own conversations and do not want to know about your troubles or gossips. Taking a call at the table is taboo. Turn your cell phone to silent or vibrator mode. Should an emergency arise, take the call outside.

SETTLING THE BILL

If you know that someone else will be picking up the bill, choose modestly. Don't be cheap. If you are footing the bill, suggest to your guests that they have free rein to order whatever they feel like. Normally, everyone at the table is served at the same time. Wait until all dishes have arrived at the table before starting. If yours is lagging behind, insist the others start. Many people these days ask for food that is not on the menu. But if you're too insistent, it can appear rude. If you are dissatisfied with the food, tell the waiter with minimal fuss, and request any necessary and reasonable changes. Keep things pleasant. Excessive complaining only spoils everyone's evening.

WHEN NO ONE REACHES FOR THE BILL

This happens when everyone was part of the decision making process to go out for a meal. Your fun dinner suddenly turns into a tricky social setting when the meal ends yet no one is reaching for the bill. If you didn't indicate that you would be treating everyone, your friends should be aware that they'd be paying for their own food. Take action and start dividing the bill or just casually ask how everyone prefers the bill to be split.

While making travel plans, always remember to do a little homework on the country you are visiting to be a little more aware of their protocol.

TIPPING

On one of my early trips to the US, my colleagues and I stepped out for dinner to a regular, not-so-fancy restaurant. After an entertaining evening, it was customary for us to split the bill, and as usual we passed on the bill to the only math whizz of the group so that he could equally divide it. He told us the amount, we all carried on to putting in our share, and then once that was done we began to walk out of the restaurant, still pretty engrossed in our own conversations. To our surprise, we were taken aback by our waiter, who suddenly burst out of the restaurant, yelling at us furiously. He went on to say that, we had not tipped him enough. We were obviously confused, and reassured him that we had in fact added the customary 10 per cent tip to our total amount. The waiter seemed to get even more enraged on hearing our response and barked back as us saying, "For your information, in America you are supposed to leave 15-20 per cent of your bill, pre-tax as a tip. Next time, before venturing out of your country, do your homework and learn how things are done here!" Mortified, we immediately tipped him a sufficient amount, apologized profusely and scurried back to our hotels.

To tip or not to tip, that is the question; and how much and to whom, is just as confusing. Proper tipping is a gesture of appreciation of services rendered, and figuring out what gratuity is appropriate is a rather complex matter that perplexes many people.

While making travel plans, always remember to do a little homework on the country you are visiting to be a little more aware of their protocol.I hope that this will help spare you the embarrassment that we had encountered.

DIFFERENT COUNTRIES, DIFFERENT NORMS

United Kingdom: In the UK, you do not tip cash in bars; appreciation for good service generally fetches the bartender a drink.

France: The French simplify matters by including a 15 per cent service charge in the bill, in most places except bars.

Japan: While tipping is customary in many countries, the opposite is the case in Japan. It's just simply not a part of Japanese culture. Either many workers get confused about why they are receiving the extra money or it can even be considered insulting or demeaning by some.

USA: America is notorious for high amount of expected tipping. Everywhere you go and anything you do, you will always have to tip. Service charge in restaurants is almost never applied to the bill (except for large parties of six people or more) so tipping between

15-25 per cent is normal.

Australia and New Zealand: Tipping is a contentious issue in Australia and New Zealand, with many locals seeing the custom as unnecessary. Many employees are still not familiar with the concept as a whole and tipping can occasionally cause some confusion. In some restaurants, employees are even forbidden to accept tips, but generally, it is acceptable to round up your bill to the nearest dollar, or to ask the employee to 'keep the change'.

Europe: In most European countries, service charges are rarely included in the bill. Debit and credit cards are widely accepted, but it's good to keep a few euros in change on hand if you're paying by card, as it's unlikely that you'll be able to add a tip through the machine. At low-end restaurants, tipping is not expected, but you can round up the bill to the nearest euro. In middle- to high-end restaurants, you can leave a few euros, up to a maximum of 5 per cent, if you were happy with the service.

The safe rule to follow would be 10-15 per cent of the total bill. This percentage basis is the best plan as it avoids under tipping. If service charge is added to the bill, there is no need to tip further. However, if the service has been extraordinary, you could leave a tip as a token of your appreciation.

If two or more waiters have served you, don't worry about dividing the tip. Restaurants have a system where tips are appropriately distributed. Leave the tip in cash on the table or add it on to your credit card bill.

In cheaper eateries in India – i.e. Udupis and fast food joints – following the percentage system also works. These restaurants cater to a lower income group who spend less time at the table as opposed to fancy restaurants who may do just one or two sittings an evening. Though the scales seem unfair, leaving Rs. 20 in these smaller eateries is an accepted practice.

In India, we are not expected to tip taxi or auto drivers. However, depending on the service, use your discretion and tip accordingly. At beauty parlours, leave 10 per cent of the bill as a tip, especially if you will be frequenting the place often. The bellhop or room service at a hotel or motel warrants a minimum tip, depending on the quality and scale of service provided. The delivery boy or errand boy deserves a minimum tip as well.

Tipping is one of the most stressful and confusing aspects of etiquette today. It is a significant way to show appreciation for a job well done. However, treating the person who has served you with respect is equally important. It begins with returning their greeting when they seat you or come over to introduce themselves. Initiate eye contact and make note of the person's name. So every time you need to call them to your table, use their name. Don't snap your fingers to get their attention, make weird sounds or wave your arms wildly so they look in your direction. If you don't remember their name, ask a passing waiter to send your server to the table as soon as possible.

When it's time to order, do so politely. Instead of saying, "I'll take the chicken kebabs and 1 butter naan," say, "May I have the chicken kebabs and 1 butter naan, please?" This also shows the children at the table how to behave. Make sure to thank your server once again when the food arrives and all the plates are on the table. You also have to thank them every time your glass of water is filled up – every time you give them any sort of instruction.

Did you know that three quarters of all restaurant-related complaints are about bad service? But that's no excuse to behave badly, believing that all are bad. If you are unhappy with the service being provided to you, do not start arguing. If the food is late in reaching your table or they got your order wrong, the server will most probably apologize. Accept the apology and ask them to rectify the problem as soon as possible. Ask to speak to the manager because he is the one who can adjust your bill or offer you a complimentary meal in the future.

Always remember...

Do your research before you travel abroad to know their tipping culture. You don't want to underpay and risk appearing like a cheap person.

If you are a large group, make a conscious effort to keep your volumes low. People tend to forget there are others around when they are having fun.

Under no circumstances should you be rude to the wait staff. Be polite even if you are angry.

5

FINE DINING

"There is a difference between dining and eating. Dining is an art. When you eat to get most out of your meal, to please the palate, just as well as to satiate the appetite that my friend, is dining."

— Yuan Mei, Chinese scholar

This is what most would consider the Holy Grail of the most sophisticated and impeccably mannered. However, even the most well-rounded person has at some point, had the misfortune of making a faux pas at the dinner table. Hopefully, it wasn't as outrageous as Peter Sellers in the riotous movie *The Party*. I have an interesting anecdote to share about something that happened to my cousin. She was at the dinner table of an aristocrat when a three-pronged silver contraption, holding a piece of lemon, caught her eye. She reached out, removed the piece of lemon from it and heartily squeezed it onto an appetizer on the table. A few moments later, the other guests picked up each of theirs and used this not so familiar looking lemon squeezer correctly. My cousin, now obviously dumbfounded and terribly embarrassed, wished someone could have briefed her. She still remembers this incident, although with a little less embarrassment, thanks to the passage of years.

Not everyone is familiar and schooled in the art of fine dining. And there's no shame in that. Not many of us have opportunities to do that on a regular basis. So all you need for a smooth sailing evening of fine dining is to keep in mind a few rules. Remember that nobody knows you are a bundle of nerves except yourself... and that's your best-kept secret. The fine dining experience can be a delightful one, which is a culinary as well as visual treat. So do try to relax and enjoy it, while minding your manners, of course.

Do try to arrive at the appointed time. This is essential, as a sit-down dinner cannot begin unless every guest has arrived.

Most soirées start with pre-dinner drinks or aperitifs. Pace yourself leisurely with the alcohol, as you will continue to be served throughout the dinner, and you don't want to end up inebriated before the end of the meal.

As you proceed to the dinner table, bear in mind that the host will have put a lot of thought into the seating arrangements. Traditionally, men and women are seated alternately. You and your spouse or dinner date could be seated separately because the whole idea is to mingle.

A small card with your name on it will specify where you are seated. And, no, you cannot swap places as that would be rude. Stand behind your designated seat and wait until the host invites everyone to take their seats. The first person to take the seat is the host of the dinner, whether it is at home or in a restaurant. If you are not sure about where to sit in the absence of place cards, wait for the host to direct you to your seat. Once seated, ensure that the first thing you do is to place your napkin on your lap. This has to be done swiftly before the maître d' arrives to do it for you. The correct way of doing so is to fold the napkin into half, with the folded side adjacent to your body. I often notice that people wait for the server or waiters to do this for them. But it's best if you do it yourself.

> Most soirées start with pre-dinner drinks or aperitifs. Pace yourself leisurely with the alcohol, as you will continue to be served throughout the dinner, and you don't want to end up inebriated before the end of the meal.

Greet the guests on either side of you and introduce yourself if you haven't met them before. In case you are seated between a Brad Pitt lookalike and a portly gentleman, try not to be biased and give both men equal attention. Never snap your fingers at the server. Just raise your hand and wave it hopefully. Don't call out.

THE TABLEWARE

The beautifully decorated table will have an array of sophisticated silverware and glassware. It might look a little intimidating at first, but don't worry. You will remember what they are for soon enough. The extra large plate placed in front of you is called a base plate. It is merely decorative and nothing should be eaten off it. Sometimes, individual menu cards stating the various dishes that will be served through the different courses are placed on top of the base plate.

A traditional fine dining meal has up to seven courses.

- Hors d'oeuvres or appetizers
- Soup
- Salad
- Sorbet (optional)
- Entrée or main course
- Cheese and fruit (optional)
- Dessert
- Coffee, tea and liqueurs

This is a typical French concept of a seven-course meal. While you may not have all the courses, a minimum of four courses is generally served at any sit-down meal. Certain courses may have vegetarian and non-vegetarian options and the server will come around to ask for your preferences. When making your choice, do make the effort to pronounce the name as written in the menu, however fanciful it may sound.

> Fine dining is about minimalistic design and elegance, so do not expect generous portions. Asking for seconds is a no-no.

People are usually flustered with the multiple forks, spoons and knives they encounter in various sizes. In fine dining, the forks are placed on the left of the plate and on the right, you will find knives and spoons. While it might look very confusing, the cutlery is arranged in order of the courses and the easiest way to remember which one to use is to work your way outwards in. Follow this rule and you are most likely not to goof up.

THE GLASSES

There will also be two or three different types of glasses. The most nondescript looking one is for water, the large rounded bowl-shaped one with a long stem is for red wine, the other slightly slender one is for white wine and then we have the elegant tall champagne flutes. If you are a teetotaller, inform the attendant and the wine glasses will be cleared off and replaced with a soft drink. Traditionally red wine is served with red meat and white wine with white meat and fish. The wines could also be changed from course to course, depending on your host's extravagance. All beverages should be served at the correct temperature. Chilled for champagne and white wine and (European) room temperature for red wine, which would be 16 to 18 degrees.

The highlight of a sit-down meal is that each dish is individually pre-plated and presented beautifully. Do not start eating until all the guests at the table have been served. The host starts the meal and then the guests follow suit. You do not have to finish everything on your plate, but you must at least taste it. This shows appreciation to the chef for the effort put in to create the dish. At all times, keep your elbows off the table. Try to maintain an upright and graceful posture and bring the food up to your mouth instead of stooping too much towards your plate. Chew with your mouth closed and resist making conversation with your mouth full. Cutlery is not a musical instrument to be clinked against your plate. All cutting and spooning should be done with minimum noise effects.

Fine dining is about minimalistic design and elegance, so do not expect generous portions. Asking for seconds is a no-no. If certain foods are difficult to fork due to their consistency, manage to take a few bites and call it quits instead of risking embarrassment. The fork is meant for picking up food only, so never scoop. Food like peas should be smashed with a knife or held steady with a knife, which you then pick up with the fork. Soup is generally served, piping hot. Please refrain from blowing at it furiously like the wolf in *Three Little Pigs*. The easier option is to spoon it from the edges of the bowl, as it tends to be cooler at the sides. Always remember that you spoon the soup away from you as you eat it. And yes, we eat our soup not drink it.

WHEN YOU ARE DONE

Another important aspect is the position of your cutlery. While you may think this is irrelevant, it actually helps to indicate whether you are still in the process of eating or if you have finished. This may be done differently in various cultures, but the most accepted way in fine dining is to place them apart in the 4 o'clock and 8 o'clock position indicating that you aren't done and when you place them together in the 6 o'clock position it signifies that you have finished your meal. The same applies to your napkin. If you need to leave the table, politely excuse yourself and place your napkin neatly folded on the chair. This indicates that you will be returning to the table and to the meal. At the end of the meal, the napkin can be left crushed at the side of your plate, which indicates that you are done.

If you do spill food or wine on yourself, do not try to clean yourself and your clothes right there while the others are eating. Instead, excuse yourself and go to the washroom. Taking phone calls in the middle of the meal is rude and disrespectful to your fellow guests, whether it's a fine dine meal or a more casual one. Have the courtesy to excuse yourself from the table if you must take the call. Ideally, your phone should be on the silent mode.

THE DESSERT

The final and most anticipated course will be dessert. The cutlery for the dessert is arranged on top of your dinner plate, depending on the place available or it could be brought in separately with the dessert. You should not eat pudding with a spoon on its own – use a spoon and a fork, or a fork on its own. When eating ice cream, use a teaspoon. Cheese and fruit, though not very popular in our country, is mandatory in most European fine dining restaurants. The traditional choices for cheese would mostly be hard cheeses like Gouda, Cheddar, Emmental or soft cheeses like Brie, Camembert. For the sharper taste buds, Roquefort and Stilton(blue cheese) may be used. The cheese board will have its own special cheese knife, which has a fork-shaped tip with two tines. Round cheese should be cut in wedges and picked up with the cheese knife. The cheese platter would generally be served with crackers, dried fruit like apricots or walnuts, and even some fresh black grapes. Usually, a sweet wine is served with this course, such as a Port. The meal will end with tea, coffee and liqueurs. Pick your choice of flavour (Crème de menthe, Cointreau, Irish Cream, Kahlúa, Drambuie, etc.).

When dining with other people, make the meal a pleasant experience for everyone at the table. They may not take offence if you accidentally use the wrong fork. But they will notice if you talk with your mouth full, chew with your mouth open, park your elbows on the table, take more food than everyone else, burp, belch and slurp, or reach across the table for something rather than asking someone to pass it to you. They will also notice if you are rude to the staff, leave the table without requesting to be excused, or, if you are a man, sit down before all the women sit first. I know of so many people who have travelled the length and breadth of the world, but eat so poorly. These are people who know how things are done, but choose to ignore them and do as they wish. They have food around their mouth while they eat; sometimes they eat with their mouth open. This really puts people off. This is why eating etiquette is so important. You don't want to make people around you uncomfortable.

I would like to end this chapter with a humorous story, the veracity of which has not been confirmed. A visiting dignitary was seated at a large dinner table with Queen Victoria. After the meal, finger bowls were placed before them. The gentleman, unsure of what it was, picked up the bowl and drank from it. The Queen, who may have actually been in utter shock, maintained her regal poise and followed suit. Simultaneously, all the other guests drank from their own finger bowls. Now that is blue-blooded table manners for you, coupled with regal courtesy. I assure you that most of us in his place would not get away with such ignorance. So while fine dining is probably the epitome of a great dining experience accompanied by much flair and style, do be sure that you have the manners and the presence of mind to match it.

The three questions that follow are the ones I have been asked the most. That's why I'd like to address them once and for all.

How do I remove pips of fruit from my mouth while still at the table?

Having seen many people trying unsuccessfully to removing pips from oranges, watermelons and other fruits from their mouth at a formal meal, I need to write about it. Most restaurants will remove the pip from the fruit before serving it to you. Don't panic, though, if you do find a pip in your mouth. It's not considered genteel to spit it into your plate. Martha Stewart, the diva of etiquette, would frown on any clumsy display at the table. Make a fist over your mouth. Pass the pip into your fist and transfer discreetly to your napkin. Or slide the pip under the plate in front of you, where it is not visible. Use your dessert spoon or fruit fork to eat your fruit at a sit-down formal lunch or dinner.

What is the correct way of using a fork and spoon? Also, how can I eat noodles in a public place if I can't use chopsticks?

Different cultures use forks and spoons in various ways. There is, however, a right way to hold cutlery. When using a spoon and fork, the spoon is held in the right hand and fork in the left. Hold the cutlery between your index finger and the thumb, pointing away from you along the line of the cutlery. The fork should be held in such a manner that the back of it – the convex curve – is towards you. The fork is used merely to steer the food into the spoon and then brought to the mouth. The food always comes up to you; you never lean towards it. Do not turn the fork over and use it as you would a spoon or scoop. At the end of the meal, place your cutlery halfway across the plate in a 6 o'clock position, facing upward, indicating you have finished.

If you are still not sure, eye someone whose table manners you respect and copy them. If you are not confident with chopsticks, follow the same rules as eating spaghetti with a fork. Twirl the fork to gather the noodles. Lightly press against the plate until it's manageable, and with a quick scooping movement gather up rolled noodles and bring to your mouth. Bite off overhanging strands in a dignified manner.

How can I relish crab and chicken legs at a restaurant without messing up?

Both the dishes are there to enjoy, but are honestly not the most dignified to eat. Crabs are served with bare shells and are expected to be eaten with your fingers. You will probably be given a nut or crab cracker to crack open the shell. Spear the meat with seafood forks or a slim, long crab spoon to tease the meat out. Soft-shelled crabs can be eaten in their entirety. Unfortunately, with most meat dishes on the bone, you are not expected to pick up the chicken leg in your fingers and chew on it. Spear the chicken part with the fork in the left hand, then, with the knife, strip the meat from the bone. No chewing. No spitting out chewed bones, no hands, unless it's an informal situation. The tiny bones can be taken in the fingers but take your lead from your host. At a less grand restaurant, if you're feeling brave, there is nothing to stop you from using your fingers, but if you are trying to be correct, you ought not to.

Always remember...

It is not necessary to finish each course, but don't offend your host by not tasting it at all.

If you are confused about the cutlery, remember the golden rule: outward in.

Take the food to your mouth. Don't bend towards the plate.

Don't forget your table manners and chew with your mouth open.

Don't speak with your mouth full and spray the person beside you.

Sip your wine or drink slowly. Large gulps are ungainly.

Elbows must always be off the table.

If you are dining at a restaurant, send your compliments to the chef.

Finally, don't forget to thank your host for a fine evening.

6

SOCIALIZING WITH BUSINESS COLLEAGUES

"I've learned that people will forget what you said, people will forget what you did, but people will never forget how you made them feel."

— Maya Angelou, American writer

t is very important to strike the right balance of professionalism and enjoyment while dining out or socializing with your boss or colleagues. You work and interact with these people on a daily basis and therefore certain decorum has to be maintained even outside the working environment. The rules that apply in the office will still hold true outside it and cannot be as relaxed when you are out with friends or acquaintances that you only meet socially.

I am not suggesting that you be a killjoy of the evening and behave like a very serious person, but at the same time you cannot let your hair down and come across as a party person. Remember that come Monday morning you have to be back in that office and you don't want people to have that inebriated wild child, unruly image of you while trying to take you seriously at work. So the key word here is balance. You should, of course, have a good time, but know your limits and stick to them.

Let's say, for example, you have finally got the big promotion that you have been working really hard for and you want to celebrate. A few questions pop into your mind:

- How do you officially invite your boss out on a Saturday evening without sounding too personal?
- What type of restaurant should you pick? Is it okay to offer drinks?

- Whom else should you invite?
- Should you be dressed for a business or social setting?

Let's start out with the invitations. It is best to invite your boss directly. Do not be coy but pleasant and professional. Say you would like to celebrate your recent success and would like to invite him and a few other colleagues to dinner. Regarding your colleagues, stick to inviting the people that you work closely with or as a team, and who may have contributed to your success.

Try to strike a gender balance in case you work in a male dominated office. Having a woman or two along will make the evening a more comfortable experience and ensure that it doesn't turn into a rowdy boys' night out. Once you have invited everyone, the next step would be to pick the appropriate restaurant. Pick a restaurant with good food that is not too pricey or fancy. Also, it is always preferable to make a reservation as you do not want your guests to be kept waiting on a busy night.

Incorporating everyone's dietary preferences would be a challenge so pick a multi-cuisine option. This way everyone can find something to suit them. Buffets are another no-hassle option, as they have a wider variety of foods to choose from. Offering drinks is completely acceptable. Getting drunk, on the other hand, is not. Your guests may take that liberty but as the host, you definitely need to be about your wits. Check with your guests what they would prefer. In case a majority of them are wine drinkers, ordering a bottle of red or white wine is a more economical option. If you are clueless about ordering wine, ask for assistance from the wine steward. In case you are worried about overspending, discreetly point at an appropriately priced wine bottle on the menu and he will get the hint. Ideally, stay away from ordering several refills and if you have a freeloader at the table, politely say you would like to move onto dinner, as most of the other people would like to start eating. A good trick is to order your

> The rules that apply in the office will still hold true outside it and cannot be as relaxed when you are out with friends or acquaintances that you only meet socially.

food immediately so that it is served as soon as possible, following the drinks.

Dressing for this evening will be as important as picking the right restaurant or ordering the right wine. While you do not need to be dressed for business, women cannot show up in a provocative outfit with ample cleavage showing either; it sends out the wrong signal. Attractive yet understated would be the way to go, as this always creates a good impression. Men should wear a crisp shirt or collared T-shirt and trousers at the dinner. You can give it a casual touch by wearing moccasins or oxfords. At the dinner table, speak softly and conduct yourself with decorum. Keep the conversation light and stick to general topics. Avoid indulging in office politics, gossip or taboo topics.

Finally, keep in mind that this is a celebration after all, so relax and enjoy yourself while projecting a professional and credible image, without having to worry about etiquette blunders.

If you are not the host but attending a business party as a guest, then pretty much the same rules apply concerning etiquette, dressing and drinking.

Always remember...

They are your office colleagues, so while you may be in a social setting, they are not your friends. Behave accordingly.

Pick a multi-cuisine restaurant because you may not know everyone's culinary choices.

7

LEISURE PROTOCOL

"It is far more impressive when others discover your good qualities without your help."

— Judith Martin, Miss Manners

The good life is here for everyone to enjoy. With ambition, development, progress and profit being top on corporate India's list, we are being pampered like never before. However, be it at a hotel on a corporate visit, or chilling out during our spare time at a cinema or a salon, the onus is also on us to behave with good conduct.

AT A HOTEL

1. Fill in the required hotel forms and make sure that you provide true information about yourself.

2. Seek local information (if required) from the correct source: the concierge will assist you with your queries or direct you accordingly.

3. Be polite with the staff and if you have a complaint to register, do so with the general manager of the hotel and again, be firm but polite.

4. Do not use hotel facilities (bar, entertainment, specialty restaurants, health club, gym, spa) if you are not authorized to do so by your company. If you do use the same, settle the payment from your personal account.

5. Maintain hygiene and etiquette standards while doing so.

6. Do not entertain personal guests when you are on business travel where your company is footing every bill.

7. Avoid any type of physical contact with any management or

staff member of the hotel.

8. Do not take away any items that take your fancy from the hotel room. These are all accounted for and the staff will be held responsible for its loss. We all have a tendency to keep some stuff we like from the room. If it's replaceable, such as toiletries in plastic bottles, it's okay to take them when you leave. I think the hotel expects everyone to do that. But stop at that. Don't take away towels and sheets. A friend once shared a story of someone she knew who flicked a painting from a five-star hotel room because he loved it. She doesn't know how he managed to bring that big thing back home on a flight. But he somehow did. I can imagine the look on the faces of the housekeeping staff when they realized the painting was missing. I was just horrified to hear that! The hotel staff stopped someone else I know who was in the lobby, as she was checking out and asked to open her luggage. They did that because they realized many things from the room were missing when she left. It was so embarrassing for me to be a witness at that scene. I cannot even imagine how she must have felt. All of that humiliation could have been avoided if she had obeyed the rules.

9. Unless it is for business, do not extend your stay to suit your fancy.

10. When on business, do not take companions, children or friends with you just so that they too can enjoy the complimentary accommodation facility.

AT THE CINEMA

1. Decide the film and show time before proceeding to the ticket counter. It's extremely impolite to waste the time of those in the queue while you make up your mind.

2. Make sure that you enter the auditorium at least five minutes before the show starts to prevent disturbing others and sit in your own seat.

3. If you are late, make your way to your seat very quietly and apologize if you step on people's feet along the way.

4. Pick up all that you want to eat before entering the auditorium

and eat as silently as possible.

5. Turn off your mobile phone and if you do need to take a call, step outside the auditorium.

6. Do not put your feet up against another seat's backrest.

7. Do not stand and block the screen view or aisles.

AT THE SALON

1. It is always better to fix an appointment, especially if you are looking forward to good, attentive service.

2. If you do fix an appointment, be on time.

3. If you are visiting the salon for a body treatment, it is always nice to have a shower, wear clean inner wear and use a mild fragrance before doing so.

4. Keep your mobile phone on the silent mode and speak softly on a call. People visit the salon for a bit of peace and loud sounds can be very annoying.

5. While all salons use fresh linen for treatments, if you are in doubt, politely ask for the towels, sheets or treatment tools to be replaced.

6. Keep your personal belongings near you and keep an eye on it as well. The salon is not responsible for its safekeeping.

7. It is always nice to ask the salon attendant who is servicing you about how they are and inquire about their well-being.

8. After settling the bill, thank the attendants who have serviced you.

9. Leave a tip of 10 per cent to 12 per cent for the main attendant and about 8 per cent to 10 per cent for the supplementary attendants, like hair washers, etc.

Whether you are at a hotel, salon or cinema, enjoy and let others do the same.

AT A HIGH TEA PARTY

There's no better time to catch up with friends than over a hot cup of tea. As you get ready to host a tea party, here's what you need to know.

Teatime entertaining was a tradition started by Anna Russell, the Duchess of Bedford, in the 17th century in England, and has over the years, become a popular practice. Contrary to popular belief, high tea was not a ceremony practised by the elite but traditionally a full meal that the working middle class would have as their evening supper, accompanied with tea.

Put someone in charge to ensure that fresh tea or coffee is served hot as and when required, and the buffet table is periodically replenished.

While the ambience and surrounding of a modern-day tea party may be different, the basic structure remains more or less the same. Send out your invitations at least a week in advance, so guests can organize their calendars. Guests, in turn, should respond promptly. It would be a good idea to follow-up with a phone call. Invite like-minded people to make it a fun and relaxed afternoon. You could have an intimate group with a few guests or a larger group, depending on the occasion.

Plan your menu taking into consideration the guests' dietary requirements (vegetarian/non-vegetarian) and the availability of the different types of teas, breads, cakes and tarts, stuffed rolls, etc. For a slightly more elaborate spread, you could include a fresh fruit salad, nuts, hot croissants and scones with clotted cream and jam.

Ensure your china and silverware is polished and the table beautifully set with pretty tea napkins and a centrepiece decorated with fresh flowers or the fruits of the season. Attention should be paid to the ambience, which would include lighting, soft background music, the correct temperature and ventilation of the room, and comfortable seating for every guest.

When the tea is served, it should be poured out by the hostess or a server. The guests should gather around the table where the buffet is set, help themselves to the food, and bring it back to where everyone is sitting. Put someone in

Your children are your responsibility all the time, even in another person's home. Discipline them if they dirty your host's house.

charge to ensure that fresh tea or coffee is served hot as and when required, and the buffet table is periodically replenished.

As far as the attire is concerned, one simple rule to follow is that you always get dressed for a tea party. However, whether you decide to go with casual chic, semiformal or formal, will depend on the type of tea party. Always check the invitation to ensure you know exactly which type of tea party you have been invited to. The dress code for a garden tea party will be different from one that is held indoors.

Conversation should be light, neutral and of general interest. Jokes and anecdotes are a part and parcel of a party as long as they are free of personal attacks and within the limits of politeness, civility and good behaviour.

Always remember...

Do not steal items from the hotel room. You have paid to board there; you don't own it.

Always turn off your cell phone or put it on vibrate mode when you are watching a movie at the cinema.

If you are hosting a tea party, always pour the first cup of tea for all your guests.

8

HOW TO BE THE PERFECT HOUSE GUEST

"Santa Claus has the right idea: visit people once a year."

– Victor Borge, Danish and American comedian

Some of my fondest memories include having guests coming over for a short stay. Perhaps, it is because our friends have lovely manners, and my husband and I enjoy making their stay memorable. But I know that this is not the experience many have had. Here are a few guidelines for being a considerate guest and a thoughtful host.

1. Be clear about when you will arrive and when you will leave, and don't go earlier or stay longer. Inform your hosts much in advance about your travel dates. And arrive and leave on those particular dates. The true houseguest from hell is someone who doesn't know when to leave.

2. Take a house gift or something that you know your host will like. If they have children, get something for them too.

3. If it's possible, have some means of transportation so you don't have to rely on your host to chauffeur you around.

4. Think of activities to occupy you for at least some part of the day. Don't expect your host to keep you entertained the entire day.

5. No matter how long you stay – whether it's a weekend or a week – offer to take your host out to dinner one evening.

6. Keep your room neat and clean up after yourself. Make your own bed each morning and keep the bathroom dry, too.

7. Offer to help with laying the table, clearing dishes, washing dishes, etc. If you have a good host, they will probably

decline. But you have to offer.

8. Don't complain about your bed, your room, the food or the outings that have been planned for your stay. Be an appreciative guest.

9. Don't ever sleep in. If the hosts get up at a particular time, you have to do that too.

10. If you are bringing children, bring plenty of toys to keep them occupied and clean up after them. Your children are your responsibility all the time, even in another person's home. Discipline them if they dirty your host's house.

11. Once you are home, send a handwritten note thanking your hosts for their hospitality. Don't wait for a month to pass before you do this. Within a day or two of your return is good enough time.

According to a survey, houseguests should always steer clear from 10 other faux pas:

1. Being on your phone over lunch/dinner
2. Asking for the wi-fi code
3. Wearing shoes on the carpet
4. Looking in bedrooms without permission
5. Looking inside the fridge without asking
6. Turning up to a dinner party without a gift
7. Helping yourself to food without asking
8. Putting your feet on the furniture
9. Turning down food when asked
10. Bringing around a pet without asking first

Always remember...

Inform your host when you will arrive and leave their home.

Always take along a gift you know your host will like and appreciate.

Clean up after yourself in their home and always offer to help them.

9

BEING A GRACIOUS HOST

"The ornaments of your home are the people who smile upon entering time and time again."

— Maralee McKee, author of *Manners That Matter for Moms*

Most of us love having guests over. While it can be a bit of a stressful time, you also have a lot of fun when friends and family comes over. If you are the one travelling, it might seem like obvious etiquette to be a gracious houseguest to whomever you are staying with. But growing up, my parents always told me that it was just as important to be a gracious host or hostess, and make your guests feel comfortable. After all, your loved ones have travelled a long way to be with you, and you want to show them how glad you are to see them. If you think of playing hostess as an inconvenience that you're going to resent even the slightest bit, it's better to say no right in the beginning. But if you do agree to host, you owe it to them to make your home as comfortable for them as possible. Make their visit a pleasure by thinking ahead and offering the same courtesies you would like to be shown. Elaborate fruit baskets and floral arrangements are not necessary, just a bit of common sense and good planning is.

Double check dates: Yes, I know you remember, but there's no harm in checking them again. Miscommunication about when your guests are arriving or leaving can start their visit off on the wrong foot. If you are picking them up at the airport or train station, make

Guests can feel awkward having to ask every time they need something. Make things easier on you and them by giving a little self-help tour early on in their stay.

sure you have all of their travel info, and agree on a place to meet.

Share your plans with them:

Let your guests know what you have planned. If you have activities in mind, tell them in advance so they can pack appropriately. This would also be a good time to check in and see if there is anything they would like to do or see while they are in town. A few years ago, we had a couple of friends over and I had planned to take them to the spa for a whole day. It was not until they arrived that they told me that one of them hates massages (strange, I know). I had to quickly changes plans. Thankfully, I had another itinerary in place.

Explain your home's quirks:

After living in your place for years, you may have forgotten how difficult it was to work the shower that first time or flush the toilet so it doesn't run all night. But your guests don't. Show them clearly how everything works so they are not inconvenienced and you know that there won't be any surprises.

Invite them to help themselves:

Guests can feel awkward having to ask every time they need something. Make things easier on you and them by giving a little self-help tour early on in their stay. Show them where you store the snacks and drinks as well as towels and toiletries. A friend was telling me this incident that happened with her daughter who had travelled to London and was staying with relatives. The host was reluctant to share some snacks that she loved and while giving my friend's daughter the tour of the house, immediately shut the cupboard that had the snacks. That is appalling behaviour!

Yes, it can be quite cumbersome to deal with unexpected visitors, especially as you are about to step out. But how wonderful it is that your friends wanted to surprise you. Hold on to that feeling even when you are irritated.

While all the above points apply to all guests, I have not covered a few scenarios yet. Let's look at a few common occurences in particular.

WHEN YOUR PARENTS INVITE GUESTS OVER

1. Clean and organize your home a couple of days in advance so your parents don't have to hurry at the last minute. On the day your guests arrive, wake up early and be ready on time. Run odd errands for groceries, etc., before the day of arrival.

2. Don't be overly demanding of your parents' attention during the course of the guest's visit.

3. Try to take care of your own responsibilities such as making your bed, fixing your breakfast or snack, leaving your parents free to attend to the guests.

4. It is not necessary to stay in the same space as the elders and be part of their conversations. But say your hellos and leave the elders to enjoy among themselves. Be promptly available when your parents call out for you.

5. Always smile, maintain a pleasant expression and speak politely to the guests, your family members and house staff.

6. Do not argue with your family members or house staff in front of the guests. If you disagree with your parents about something, don't voice it in front of the guests. You can discuss it after they are gone or when you are alone with your parents.

7. If your routine or schedule is curbed by the visit, discuss it with your parents and find a way to be accommodating; after all, it is only temporary.

8. Most importantly, even if you don't like the guests, allow your parents to be as welcoming and hospitable as they want to.

WHEN A GUEST ARRIVES AS YOU ARE LEAVING HOME

1. Let the guest know that the entire family has a prior commitment that has to be honoured, but that you will take a few minutes to get them comfortable until you return.

2. Show them to the room they will be occupying and provide them with bath linen and toiletries.

3. Explain that while a meal may not be possible at such short

notice, they can help themselves to some snacks or give them takeaway menus.

4. Explain the security instructions of the house and tell them of the time of your return.

5. Request them not to answer the telephone or open the door, as they are not likely to know what to do about the caller.

6. Leave your contact number so you can be reached in case of an emergency.

WHEN THEY DROP IN TO SAY HELLO

1. Yes, it can be quite cumbersome to deal with unexpected visitors, especially as you are about to step out. But how wonderful it is that your friends wanted to surprise you. Hold on to that feeling even when you are irritated.

2. Let the guests in politely; inform them that you are on your way out and that you only have time for a quick refreshment. This will let them know that this is not a good time and hopefully, they will make a quick exit.

3. If you cannot spare the time for refreshments, apologize and request them to call the next day to schedule a planned visit or offer to drop in yourself.

4. Thank them for coming and see them off at the door.

Always remember...

For the duration of your guests' stay, your home is practically their home. Make them feel welcome.

Tell them how everything in your house works, such as bathroom knobs, and where the food and drinks are stored, so they can help themselves.

If your parents have friends who are visiting, drop by and say hello. Don't confine yourself to your room.

If guests drop by without informing you, ask them to come back later.

10

HOW TO BE A SAVVY TRAVELLER

"The worst thing about being a tourist is having other tourists recognize you as a tourist."

— Russell Baker, American writer

A s world travellers, we have a responsibility and obligation to maintain respect for people, places and things. Unfortunately, at times, we are unable to choose our travel companions and we may be thrown together, for long spells of time, on nonstop journeys. In such instances, consideration for your fellow travellers is of paramount importance. However, in the eventuality that you have an unfortunate encounter with an inconsiderate fellow traveller, you needn't just grin and bear it. A large dollop of diplomacy could help. Here are a few suggestions to help make your journey pleasant. It starts with the airplane.

1. Fight the urge to jump queues. We all want to do that and not waste our time standing in line and waiting our turn. But don't! Treat flight attendants with respect. Never demand, always ask. As a former flight attendant, I have had countless experiences with ill-mannered passengers. Just because it's their job to serve you, doesn't mean that they have to be at your beck and call all the time.

2. It's always a good idea to warn the person in the row behind you if you plan to recline your chair. I was once having a meal when the person in front of me, probably wanting to sleep, reclined his seat without asking me. Some of the food spilled on my lap. Thankfully, it was a short flight and I was on my way home.

3. The washroom is the most frequented part of a plane or train.

Don't fall asleep in there. Be considerate to the normally long queues of people waiting outside. Use the sink and toilet bowl with care and wipe it dry for the next person. Don't clog the commode with toilet paper or wet the surrounding.

4. Speak softly. Sound carries, especially in an airplane. If you are chatting with friends, be mindful of volume so that you don't disturb others who might be trying to work or sleep. If you are bored and want to talk to your neighbour, test the waters before you launch into an animated conversation or make friendly overtures. If you are receiving monosyllabic answers, take the hint and read a magazine instead. If, on the other hand, a chatterbox plagues you, politely say you are feeling sleepy and pretend to sleep.

5. Proper etiquette should also extend to boarding and disembarking from the plane. Before takeoff, this means obeying boarding zone rules and being mindful of using only the overhead bin space above your seat. I had a nasty experience once where a fellow traveller behaved in a very selfish manner. I remember my excitement quickly evaporated when an inconsiderate fellow traveller left me with my neck in a brace through my long-awaited vacation last year. While landing in Paris once, an impatient traveller opened the overhead bin while the seat belt sign was on. The lurching plane sent a heavy bag crashing on my head, spraining my neck. The man scooted without even apologizing. I had to spend my entire vacation in a neck brace. After landing, it means waiting your turn to get out of your seat and retrieve your belongings, then moving quickly towards exit. Let passengers who have to take connecting flights disembark first.

> The washroom is the most frequented part of a plane or train. Don't fall asleep in there. Be considerate to the normally long queues of people waiting outside.

When you are travelling abroad, you have to follow that country's rules. That's not to say that the way you do something is wrong. But respecting cultural differences is important. You wouldn't like it if a guest entered your home with shoes on, would you? Then why would you not do things the way the locals do it in their country? It's a way of showing that you respect their culture. We – my fellow flight attendants and me – once went to a souk in Saudi Arabia during a layover. A few of the crew members came there wearing sleeveless and backless clothes because it was a very hot day. That was inappropriate and probably offensive. I could see that even the women there scorned at them. Find out about the culture of a place before you visit.

Medical treatments and medication outside India are expensive. It would do good to carry the basics (anti-allergens, vitamins, etc.) with you as well as any special ones prescribed by your doctor if you suffer from or are prone to any environmental or food allergies.

I was once flying from India with a foreign crew. Not everyone is a seasoned traveller; many times, it is the passenger's first flight. We all know that flying can be intimidating, especially when you don't speak English. And a flight attendant has to make all passengers feel at ease. The air hostess, after the meal, was on the tea and coffee round. But one of the passengers was probably too shy to speak and did the Indian head bobble, where we move the head from side to side, not indicating clearly if we're saying yes or no to a question. This irritated the air hostess and she angrily poured both coffee and tea into his cup. Now that was just rude. She should have been sensitive to the passenger's discomfort with English and not behaved as she did. As an international high-flyer, it was her job to know about basic cultural differences and she failed miserably.

WHEN TRAVELLING ON BUSINESS

Travelling for work is not the same as leisure travel. Although there are similarities, when you are travelling for business, you represent your company and its culture, not just yourself. If you are rude or are overly casual toward the hotel staff, it can have a negative impact on your company.

Dress appropriately: What you wear during a business trip speaks volumes about you and your company. If you dress too casually, it may be considered disrespectful. And you risk the chance that the person you're meeting won't take you seriously. Plan your wardrobe ahead while making a note of what you will wear during the day and in the evening. During your travels, don't wear anything you would not wear to work.

Be punctual: Punctuality is one of the most important keys to success in business. In fact, arriving early for business meetings is always a good idea. This allows you to get ready to work on schedule. Schedule your departure times and appointments wisely. Give yourself extra time to catch a connecting flight or freshen up before each appointment.

Follow social rules: Good table manners are more crucial at business meetings. Follow your host's leads and take cues from them when ordering, eating, relaxing and talking. Also, avoid using your phone to check emails or answer a call when you are with your host.

Research the city's culture: As a courtesy, study and learn about the local customs and cultural practices of the place you are visiting. If you are travelling outside India, brush up on the country's gifting customs, negotiating styles, use of names and titles, and behaviour norms of the local people such as punctuality, communication and social structure.

Always behave professionally: Remember that you are there for business. You can have fun, but no matter what your companions are doing, you are not travelling for relaxation. Avoid getting too familiar, particularly with your boss, and never drink too much.

WHEN TRAVELLING ALONE

Travelling is a thrill and travelling alone is an even bigger thrill because you can choose to do as you please. Whether it's conducting business, sightseeing, shopping or simple wandering, you can do all if that without the worry of how the others feel. However, you may want to observe a few precautions while travelling out of the country. Let's focus around the classic destinations of the United Kingdom, the United States of America and South East Asia.

Get your basics right: For starters, take care to choose that one small bag that will carry your passport, traveller's cheques and travel documents. Avoid typically backpacker gear or stuff that would make you stand out as a tourist to avoid touts and other forms of local harassment.

Ensure that your passport is valid and has a few blank pages before you proceed to make any visa applications. The applications may not be processed if both of the above conditions do not comply. Once you have received your visa, take two sets of photocopies of your passport and ticket. Keep one at home and travel with the other in your handbag. This will come in handy in case of theft or loss of the original.

Do not give away details of your accommodation, credit cards or the fact that you are travelling alone.

Take out travel insurance, especially if you are headed West, as this will safeguard you.

If you are headed to the USA, luggage is restricted in terms of size; ensure that your airline provided you with the accurate information.

Keep the weather in mind when packing your toiletries, clothing and footwear. Popular Far Eastern destinations boast of a weather that is quite like that of coastal India, although some countries like Singapore may have unexpected rain showers throughout the year. Hong Kong, on the other hand, is colder in the evenings, especially in the months of October to March. Different cities and states in the UK and USA would vary, so make sure you're well informed of the same when planning your travel.

Accordingly, it would do good to carry an overcoat, a wrap or cardigan, both for day and night wear, and appropriate footwear like boots, body lotions, lip balms etc.

Accordingly, pack clothes and take care to dress with caution in places like Kuala Lumpur, as it is predominantly Islamic. While the Western countries are more accommodating, be careful to avoid unnecessary attention when you are alone.

It is advisable for the men to wear a sports jacket or a blazer, especially in the evening, as you never know where you may want to land up for a drink.

Medical treatments and medication outside India are expensive. It would do good to carry the basics (anti-allergens, vitamins, etc.) with you as well as any special ones prescribed by your doctor if you suffer from or are prone to any environmental or food allergies.

Be sensible and carry your mobile phone. Remove the Indian SIM card and once at your destination, find the most economical mobile phone service and use it. Calls, especially, out of the USA, are very expensive but locally available calling cards come much cheaper.

Carry a diary of important telephone numbers, both that of home ground and that of the travel destination – travel agent, doctor, family for emergency, Indian Embassy or Consulate, hotel, car rental service and local doctor. These nuggets of information can be researched prior to travel or may be obtained from the concierge desk at your hotel.

Choose your accommodation wisely: For the women especially, choose a decent accommodation that is located near civil habitation and has a well-lit approach. Opt for the all-women's floor that hotels are promoting for safely. Walk through the lobby level and your floor, and make a mental note of the emergency exits.

While men too can choose to take such precautions, they may perhaps choose accommodations closest to commuting points – bus stations, underground or the subway. When travelling alone, one is bound to strike up conversation with people around, but do make sure that you do not provide any information that may in any way jeopardize your safety either at the destination or on home ground.

Do not give away details of your accommodation, credit cards or the fact that you are travelling alone.

When in doubt of finding your way around, ask the local police who you will always find at traffic lights and main streets. Avoid walking through bylanes especially after dark.

Respect cultural differences: The Americans are a more gregarious lot so being a little effusive and casual with them works, but the English are rather reserved so ask for exactly what you want and be on your way.

The people in the South East Asian countries also tend to be reserved and have a tendency to be soft-spoken. Seek your information with the same demeanour as any other may offend them.

Another difference is that the people in the South East Asian regions do not point their fingers to indicate directions as it is considered rude, they use their fist with the thumbs folded over on the top. So watch that finger!

While the English tend to be more gregarious around pubs and nightclubs, restaurant visits for meals are a much quieter affair, far from what you may see in the USA or South East Asia. So adopt the best-suited demeanour when eating out.

Always remember...

Respect the culture and the people of the place you are visiting.
Don't rush to exit the aircraft. It's just plain rude.
When travelling for business, always stay professional.
If you are travelling alone, be aware of your surroundings at all times so that you don't risk your safety.

11

CIVIC SENSE & SENSIBILITY

"He longed for cleanliness and tidiness: it was hard to find peace in the middle of disorder."

– Robin Hobb, *City of Dragons*

I am sure you all agree with me when I say that all of us are responsible for the environment that we inhabit and that the government agencies are just the means to assist us in executing that responsibility. Here are a few pointers to help us identify and address our sense of civility towards our environment.

Keep it personal: Spitting, urinating and defecating in public places are a big no – these are best done in the privacy of our bathrooms. Besides the fact that it is shameless to be doing so, it also pollutes the environment. Don't you think that our cities will soon resemble a huge garbage dump? And if we do not take action in our own individual way, we can kiss good health and well-being goodbye. Please do not litter the streets, cinemas, our seafront and beaches, places of worship... litter has a place of its own and it is called the dustbin.

Road sense: Apart from that, it has become a menace to walk on our roads today because when we do, how many of us do so without risking our lives as well as the lives of the drivers of automobiles? We can continue to blame rash driving and drivers, but as pedestrians, we also carry a responsibility to walk on the footpath and check for traffic before we cross.

Of course, when it comes to the drivers, there's a lot that they can assist with too. Maintaining driving lanes and not driving on the opposite side of the road or in the middle, not honking relentlessly, parking close enough to the curb and not in a way that causes traffic jams, and not stopping in the middle of the road to get in and out the automobiles.

Chivalry is cool: Chivalry and sensitivity can come in the form of assisting old people, children and women wherever and whenever required – while crossing the streets, at payment booths, in public transport, and at places of leisure and entertainment. Let them go ahead of you, offer them your seats, help to carry their bags if they have any. All this goes a long way in defining the fabric of our people.

Sound check: Volume control is another menace and world health bodies are now studying this as a form of pollutant. So don't honk your horns unnecessarily. Please speak softly over the telephone, especially when you have company and at public places, and keep the volume of the music in your car, homes, restaurants, and bars to an audible level. There is a reason the mobile phone was invented. Please carry the instrument when you leave your workstation, or keep it on silent when you need to step out for a break. It is very annoying for co-workers to have to listen to your favourite ringtone – a popular hit song or the goo-goo sounds of your one-year-old.

> There is a reason the mobile phone was invented. Please carry the instrument when you leave your workstation, or keep it on silent when you need to step out for a break.

Be on time: A sense of consideration also applies to time. It is important to keep the assigned time for all activities – for personal and professional meetings, for delivery of services, for completion of assignments.

Every responsible and considerate citizen of our country must also deliver this sense of discipline to their domestic and professional support staff – the house help, cooks, chefs at eateries, drivers, errand boys, delivery boys. We need to do this together. Tip them well, and do not deny them their quota of annual paid leave.

Always remember...

Do not litter anywhere. Carry a small plastic bag with you at all times and put your waste in it. Once you reach home, you can dispose of it.

Observe lane rules while driving so you don't cause accidents and endanger lives.

It's best to reach any place before time. Keep the traffic situation in your city in mind before you leave home.

ACKNOWLEDGEMENTS

Think about any question you've had regarding the hows of human interaction and the answer is always the same. Etiquette. It is the bedrock of basic human behavior and the key to a kinder, nicer world.

This book is a labour of love that comes straight from my heart. I live by the rules in this book and wanted to share my knowledge with those who are eager to imbibe it.

I thank my commissioning editor Reena Jayswal for her support, direction and input, which have made this book what it is. Thanks to Abhishek Parekh at Jaico for approaching me to write this book, the contents of which would have otherwise remained in the recesses of my mind.

My heartfelt thanks to all those who have helped me in my writing efforts: Vinifer Mehta, Parita Patel, Cyrus Merchant.

My deepest gratitude to my mother, the strongest person I know, my sister Diane, my confidante and critique, and my family and close friends who have been my pillars of strength.

Last but not the least, thank you to my beloved husband Mustafa and daughter Zara for their encouragement in this endeavor and for believing in me.

I hope this book helps bring a bit more kindness, love and good manners into the world, so that our journeys here are more pleasant ones.